PROJECT PLANNING AND SCHEDULING

The books in the Project Management Essential Library series provide project managers with new skills and innovative approaches to the fundamentals of effectively managing projects.

Additional titles in the series include:

Managing Projects for Value, John C. Goodpasture

Effective Work Breakdown Structures, Gregory T. Haugan

Managing Project Quality, Timothy J. Kloppenborg and Joseph A. Petrick

Project Measurement, Steve Neuendorf

Project Estimating and Cost Management, Parviz F. Rad

Project Risk Management: A Proactive Approach, Paul S. Royer

www.managementconcepts.com

PROJECT PLANNING AND SCHEDULING

Gregory T. Haugan

MANAGEMENTCONCEPTS

Vienna, Virginia

(((
MANAGEMENTCONCEPTS
8230 Leesburg Pike, Suite 800
Vienna, VA 22182
(703) 790-9595
Fax: (703) 790-1371
www.managementconcepts.com

Printed in the United States of America

Library of Congress Cataloging-in-Publication Data
Haugan, Gregory T., 1931–
    Project planning and scheduling/Gregory T. Haugan.
        p. cm.—(Project management essential library)
    Includes bibliographical references and index.
    ISBN 1-56726-136-1 (pbk)
      1. Project management. 2. Production planning. 3. Production scheduling.
    I. Title. II. Series.

HD69.P75 H378 2002
658.4'04—dc21
                                                                    2001054377

Although none of its material has been used *per se*, this book makes references to
the *Project Management Body of Knowledge* (*PMBOK® Guide*); therefore, the Project
Management Institute (PMI®) has requested we provide a disclaimer that PMI® did
not participate in the development of this book and has not reviewed its content
for accuracy. PMI® does not endorse or otherwise sponsor this book and makes
no warranty, guarantee, or representation, expressed or implied, as to its accuracy
or content. PMI® does not have any financial interest in this book and has not
contributed any financial resources.

About the Author

Gregory T. Haugan, Ph.D., PMP, has been a Vice President with GLH Incorporated for the past 16 years, specializing in project management consulting and training. He has more than 40 years of experience as a consultant and as a government and private sector official in the planning, scheduling, management, and operation of projects of all sizes, as well as in the development and implementation of project management and information systems.

Dr. Haugan is an expert in the application and implementation of project management systems. He participated in the early development of WBS and C/SCS (earned value) concepts at DoD and in the initial development of PERT cost software. He was the Martin Marietta representative on the Joint Army Navy NASA Committee developing the initial C/SCS concepts. He is particularly expert in the areas of scope management, cost management and schedule management, setting up new projects, and preparing proposals.

Dr. Haugan received his Ph.D. from the American University, his MBA from St. Louis University, and his BSME from the Illinois Institute of Technology.

*I dedicate this book
to
Cindy, Susan, Gregory
Charles, and Joanne*

Table of Contents

Foreword

One of the most significant contributions to general management theory and practice has been the development of the field of project management that evolved from the work in the 1960s by the Department of Defense (DOD) and the aerospace and construction industries. Although the father of scheduling is acknowledged to be Henry Gantt, from his work prior to World War II, many additional tools and techniques to assist project managers are of more recent vintage. Primary among these are the network planning algorithms known as PERT, CPM, and PDM, and the subsequent project management software that significantly improved the ability to develop effective plans and schedules.

Dr. Gregory T. Haugan, the author of this book, was one of the people who participated actively in the development of project management from the beginning as a user, developer, and trainer. In the early 1960s, he moved from an engineering position at McDonnell Aircraft Company into a planning position using PERT. He subsequently moved to the Central Planning Staff at Martin Marietta, and then managed major projects at the U.S. Department of Transportation.

As President of GLH, Incorporated, I have been directly acquainted with Dr. Haugan's work in this area and see where his many years of practical experience have been incorporated into this book.

Project Planning and Scheduling fills a long-standing need for a comprehensive yet practical description of the tools of project planning and scheduling and their application. Effective time management is the key to successful project management, and this book is an essential means toward that end.

Dr. Ginger Levin

Preface

This book is designed to provide an overview of current planning techniques and specific information on the details of project planning for project managers or project planners. It is organized into five sections:

1. **Introduction to Project Planning and Scheduling**—Purpose and role of planning and the relationship to the *PMBOK® Guide.*
2. **Concepts and Tools of Planning and Scheduling**—Different types of planning and scheduling tools and their applications.
3. **Steps in Project Planning and Scheduling**—Seven major steps in establishing a baseline plan, schedule, and detailed information that should be in a project plan.
4. **Advanced Planning and Scheduling Considerations**—Optimization and resource heuristics, critical chain project management, and project management maturity models.
5. **Summary and Checklist**—Checklist to assist the project manager in the development of project plans and schedules using project management software.

The text is followed by a bibliography and an index.

This book is a product of my 40 years of project management experience, including participating as the Martin Company (later Martin Marietta, now Lockheed Martin) representative to a government/industry task force in the 1960s, when many of the project management tools now in daily use throughout the world were first developed. As a project manager, consultant, and mentor to project managers, and as a trainer and course developer, I have been involved in developing a large number of plans and schedules; much of this experience is reflected in this book.

Thanks goes to the staff and editors of Management Concepts, Inc., and my business partner, Dr. Ginger Levin, who encouraged me in this endeavor and provided many useful editorial and substantive comments.

Gregory T. Haugan

CHAPTER 1

Introduction to Project Planning and Scheduling

Many people and organizations do not manage time well. If time is managed well, other factors are much easier to manage, and projects will be more effective and efficient. Lack of time management can and probably will result in failure of the project. Time management, therefore, is crucial to project success. In fact, many years of project management experience have demonstrated over and over that an integrated project plan and schedule is the single most important factor in project success.

> *It is not possible to control costs if the schedule is slipping; if the schedule slips, product performance is at risk if costs are held constant.*

DEFINITIONS

The world of project management is full of jargon and acronyms. The purpose of this section is to provide a set of definitions of the most common project management terms used frequently in this book. Most of these definitions are commonly used in the project management field and are also included in similar form in the Glossary of the Project Management Institute's *Guide to the Project Management Body of Knowledge*, known as the *PMBOK® Guide*.[1] This document and its role in project management are discussed later in the section Planning, Scheduling, and the *PMBOK® Guide*.

THE PURPOSE OF PLANNING

The dictionary has several definitions of "plan" and "planning." For our purposes, the most relevant one is: "any detailed method, formulated beforehand, for doing or making something."[2] "Planning" is the process of establishing objectives and determining beforehand the best way of achieving those objectives. The dictionary also lists the word "project" as a synonym for "plan" and goes on to state: "project implies the use of enterprise or

Key Definitions

Definitions for frequently used terms that relate directly to planning and scheduling concepts include:

Activity: An element of work performed during the course of a project. An activity normally has an expected duration, cost, and resource requirements. Activities have defined beginnings and endings. The terms "activity" and "task" are frequently used interchangeably, but activity is preferred and is used in this book.

Deliverable: Any measurable, tangible, verifiable outcome, result, or item that must be produced to complete a project or part of a project. All work packages and most activities have output products that can be referred to as deliverables. The term is commonly used more narrowly in reference to an external deliverable, which is a deliverable that is subject to approval by the project sponsor or customer.

Milestone: (1) A significant event in the project, usually completion of a major deliverable; or (2) a clearly identifiable point in a project or set of activities that commonly denotes a reporting requirement or completion of a large or important set of activities.

Plan: An intended future course of action.

Program: A group of related projects managed in a harmonized way. Programs may include an element of ongoing work until the lifecycle of the program is completed.

Project: A temporary endeavor undertaken to create a unique product, service, or result.

Project Schedule: The planned dates for performing activities and meeting milestones. Schedules or related portions of schedules list activity start or completion dates in chronological order.

Task: A generic term for the lowest level of defined effort on a project; often used interchangeably with the term "activity." Tasks are sometimes used to define a further breakdown of activities.

Work Breakdown Structure: A deliverable-oriented grouping of project elements that organizes and defines the total work scope of the project in a hierarchical structure. Each descending (or "child") level represents an increasingly detailed definition of the project work, and the set of child elements under a "parent" includes 100 percent of the work represented by the parent element.

Work Package: The lowest level work element in the work breakdown structure, which provides a logical basis for defining activities or assigning responsibility to a specific person or organization.

imagination in formulating an ambitious or extensive plan (they've begun work on the housing *project*)." Also, according to the dictionary, the word "plan" is derived from a French word meaning "earlier." The key words here are "beforehand" and "earlier." A plan is something you prepare prior to the work to achieve specific objectives.

The same dictionary defines the noun "schedule" as "a timed plan for a procedure or project" and the verb "schedule" as "to appoint or plan for a certain time or date."

Planning is therefore the process of determining in advance the work to be done on a project, and scheduling is assigning specific times or dates to the work. Why a project manager should plan is another question. Three answers follow:

1. Koontz and O'Donnell explain it very concisely: "Planning is to a large extent the job of making things happen that would not otherwise occur." They go on to state: "Planning is thus an intellectual process, the conscious determination of courses of action, the basing of decisions on purpose, facts, and considered estimates."[3]

2. The Cheshire Cat in *Alice's Adventures in Wonderland* has another, but similar response:[4]

   "Cheshire-Puss, would you tell me, please, which way I ought to go from here?"
   "That depends a good deal on where you want to get to," said the Cat.
   "I don't much care where—" said Alice.
   "Then it doesn't matter which way you go," said the Cat.
   "—As long as I get somewhere," Alice added as an explanation.
   "Oh, you're sure to do that," said the Cat, "if you only walk long enough."
   Alice felt that this could not be denied.

   Like Koontz and O'Donnell, the Cat suggests that if you want to get somewhere in particular, you need to know where it is and prepare a plan to achieve it.

3. A plan provides the basis for control. Without a plan, there is no basis for determining when variances occur and no basis for any corrective action. If it makes no difference which path Alice takes, then no control is needed, and eventually she will get "somewhere."

There are three purposes of planning: (1) to think out the steps that should be taken to achieve an objective, (2) to give direction to the persons working on the project to help ensure that they are synchronized in working toward the same objective, and (3) to provide a basis for identifying variances so that you can take corrective action when necessary.

However, there are several reasons that more and better planning and scheduling are not performed:

1. **Laziness**: It is often more fun or interesting to start working than to sit down and plan.
2. **To avoid accountability**: If there is plan, there is no basis for measuring performance.
3. **Inability**: Some people have difficulty thinking out the logical steps in a process.
4. **Ignorance**: Some people may not know how to plan and schedule.

The first two items are management and internal discipline problems, and the third is a characteristic of some otherwise valuable project team member that needs to be worked around. The fourth is the purpose of this book—to provide a basis for developing plans and schedules.

When people are part of a planning effort, they develop ownership of at least a part of the results. This internalization is constructive and, perhaps more than any other single activity, builds a strong project team with a desire to have a successful project.

If they were not part of making the plan, they might not want to be part of executing the plan!

The work breakdown structure, Gantt charts, and activity networks are the key tools used in the planning and scheduling of projects. These will be discussed in turn.

PLANNING AND SCHEDULING IN THE PROJECT MANAGEMENT PROCESS

Managing projects is a continuous process. Figure 1-1 illustrates the basic project management process. It focuses on achieving the project objectives within the project management triple constraint of time-cost-quality (performance).

Each of the ten steps has a specific output that is defined and documented. The steps are frequently iterative, that is, circumstances that arise in accomplishing later steps may require revision of an earlier step and subsequent repetition of all or part of the succeeding steps. This constant iteration and replanning characterize the day-to-day activities of the project manager and the project team.

The basic project management process has five phases or types of activities: initiation, planning, executing, controlling, and closing, as illustrated

FIGURE 1-1   Basic Project Management Process

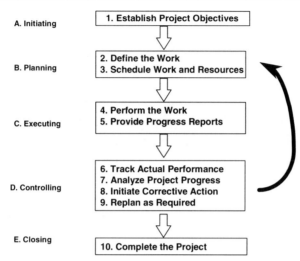

in Figure 1-1. This categorization emphasizes the importance of planning before extensive project work begins and of bringing the project to closure once all the work is done.

Because project management is a process with feedback loops, whenever the information system that collects the data for Step 6 and the analysis conducted during Step 7 indicate an adverse variance, the process is repeated for those portions of the project that are affected. This may include one or more steps of the planning phase and perhaps a rethinking of the initiation phase.

PLANNING, SCHEDULING, AND THE *PMBOK® GUIDE*

The lead in monitoring and documenting project management practices transitioned from the public to the private sector in the 1980s with the reductions in the space program, the end of the Cold War, and the rapid growth of the public sector's awareness of the importance of formal project management.

The Project Management Institute (PMI®), a professional association of more than 70,000 members, through its conferences, chapter meetings, monthly magazine *PMNetwork*, and quarterly journal, provides a forum for the growth and development of project management practices. In August 1987, PMI® published a landmark document, *The Project Management Body of Knowledge*, which was followed in 1996 by *A Guide to the Project Management Body of Knowledge*. This was last updated in 2000.[5] The *PMBOK*®

Guide reflects the 30 years of experience gained in project management since the seminal work of the U.S. Department of Defense (DOD), the National Aeronautics and Space Administration (NASA), other government organizations, and the aerospace industry in the 1960s.

The *PMBOK® Guide* documents proven traditional practices that are widely applied as well as knowledge of innovative and advanced practices that have seen more limited use but are generally accepted. The material in this book is consistent with the material contained in the *PMBOK® Guide*.

The *PMBOK® Guide* is not intended to be a "how-to" document, but instead provides a structured overview and basic reference to the concepts of the profession of project management. The *PMBOK® Guide* focuses on the project management processes. Planning and scheduling are addressed in the *PMBOK® Guide* in two sections: Project Integration Management and Project Time Management.

NOTES

1. *PMBOK®* is a trademark of the Project Management Institute, Inc., which is registered in the United States and other nations.
2. *Webster's New World Dictionary of the American Language, College Edition* (New York: The World Publishing Company, 1966).
3. Harold Koontz and Cyril O'Donnell, *Principles of Management*, 2nd edition (New York: McGraw-Hill Book Company, Inc., 1959), p. 453.
4. Lewis Carroll, *The Complete Works of Lewis Carroll* (New York: The Modern Library, Random House, 1922), p. 71.
5. *A Guide to the Project Management Body of Knowledge (PMBOK® Guide)* (Newtown Square, PA: Project Management Institute, 2000).

CHAPTER 2

Concepts and Tools of Planning and Scheduling

The term "planning" is so broad, as reflected in the dictionary definition mentioned earlier, that it invites miscommunication when referring to the activity. Dr. Robert N. Anthony analyzed this issue and suggests a framework for discussing and analyzing planning and control systems.[1] He describes three types of planning that occur in an organization: strategic planning, management control, and operational control.

Strategic planning is defined as the process of deciding on objectives of the organization, changes to these objectives, the resources to attain these objectives, and the policies that are to govern the acquisition, use, and disposition of these resources.[2] This type of planning is done at the upper levels of the organization and guides the direction of the organization as a whole.

The next type of planning, which is associated with the ongoing administration of the enterprise, is called *management control* (as a simplified version of "management planning and control"). Management control is the process by which managers ensure that resources are obtained and used effectively and efficiently to accomplish the organization's objectives.[3] The term "control" is not used in the narrow sense of ensuring that operations conform to plans, but rather that resources are used effectively and efficiently. This type of planning includes formulating budgets, establishing advertising campaigns, deciding on plant rearrangement, formulating decision rules for operational control, deciding on projects, and planning projects.

Management control systems are constructed around a financial core in the operation of a business, as dollars are the common denominator for the heterogeneous elements of inputs and outputs. Projects fall within Anthony's definition of management control systems but also are subject to the triple constraint of resources, time, and performance.

The third type of planning is called *operational control*, again as a contraction of the term "operational planning and control." Operational control is the process of ensuring that specific activities are carried out effectively and efficiently.[4] It includes such activities as controlling hiring, implementing policies, controlling placement of advertising, controlling inventory, and developing production schedules. It assumes that exact data will be available and is deterministic as compared to management control, which uses approximations.

Operational control system data often consist of non-monetary metrics such as number of items or hours, pounds of waste, machine-minutes, and person-minutes. There are elements of operational control in many project activities, especially in non-labor categories. Schedule control has many aspects of operational control, especially as practiced in some organizations after the schedule is "baselined."

In our context, project and program planning fits under management control, but with some overlap, as shown in the Venn diagram in Figure 2-1.

Project planning and scheduling is not an exact process, like a production facility turning out thousands of identical products each day, although certain activities can be planned and managed operationally. For the most part, our metrics are not precise, all projects are unique, and management judgment is required for planning and control.

Projects must relate to the overall strategy of the organization, and the project can affect the strategy and in turn be affected by changes in strategies. Our goal is to complete the project successfully and deliver the product, service, or result to our customers for their use and benefit.

Figure 2-2 presents a hierarchy of the major planning and control systems.

STRATEGIC PLANNING

Strategic planning is defined as the process of deciding on objectives of the organization, changes to these objectives, the resources to attain these

FIGURE 2-1   Three Types of Planning and Control Systems

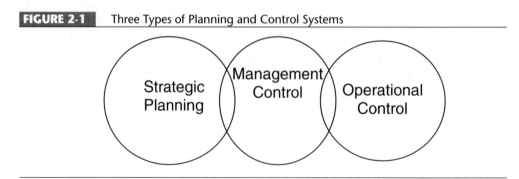

FIGURE 2-2   Planning and Scheduling Entity Hierarchy

Level 1	Level 2	Level 3	Level 4	Level 5
1. STRATEGIC PLANNING	1. Applied Strategic Planning	Various Methodologies[1]		
	2. Enterprise-Wide Resource Planning (ERP)	Software models tailored to the business		
2. MANAGEMENT CONTROL	1. Enterprise Project Management Systems	1. Enterprise Project Management		
		2. Portfolio Management		
	2. Program	1. Lifecycle Phases		
		2. Multiple Projects		
	3. Project	1. Project Charter		
		2. Gantt Chart		
		3. Milestone Chart		
		4. Network Planning	1. PERT CPM/PDM	1. PERT
				2. CPM—Arrow Diagram
				3. PDM
			2. GERT	GERT Network
			3. Critical Chain	Critical Chain Network
		5. Project Plan	Subsidiary Plans	
3. OPERATIONAL CONTROL	1. Materiel Resource Planning (MRP)	• Bills of Material • MRP Planning and Scheduling • Purchasing Management • Inventory Management • Manufacturing Order Management		
	2. Line of Balance			

1. For example, see Leonard Goodstein, Timothy Nolan, and J. William Pfeiffer, *Applied Strategic Planning: A Comprehensive Guide* (San Diego: Pfeiffer & Co., 1992).

objectives, and the policies that are to govern the acquisition, use, and disposition of these resources.

There are many different types of strategic plans—probably as many as there are organizations that do strategic planning. The common denominators are the display format, which is usually a written document, and the goal of providing long-term guidance to the organization.

Applied Strategic Planning Model

Applied strategic planning is the process by which the leaders of the organization envision its future and develop the necessary procedures and operations to achieve that future. To be effective, the leaders must ensure that the strategic plans become the basis for decision-making and management decisions at all levels.

Figure 2-3 presents a generic version of the applied strategic planning model as presented by Goodstein, Nolan, and Pfeiffer.[5]

The steps in the process can be briefly described as follows:

1. **Planning to plan**: Clarify expectations, obtain management commitment, establish the planning team.
2. **Values review**: Establish stakeholder values and the culture and philosophy of the organization.
3. **Mission formulation**: Develop a statement of what business the organization is in or plans to be in, for whom the organization performs this business, how it fills this function, and why this organization exists.
4. **Strategic business modeling**: Define in detail the paths by which the organization's mission is to be accomplished, critical success factors, strategic thrusts, and supporting culture.

These steps are all related to the organization's future and where it wants to go. The next steps determine what the organization's capabilities are and what they need to improve:

5. **Performance audit**: Develop a clear understanding of the organization's current performance and perform a SWOT (strengths, weaknesses, opportunities, and threats) analysis.
6. **Gap analysis**: Identify the gaps between the current performance of the organization and the desired performance required for the successful realization of the strategic business model direction. For each gap that cannot be closed by a specific strategy, the planning team must return to the strategic business modeling step and rethink the model until the gap can be closed.

Once the strategic business modeling, performance audit, and gap analyses are in balance, the next steps can proceed. This set of steps represents a reality check to ensure that the desires of the organization can be met:

FIGURE 2-3   Applied Strategic Planning Model

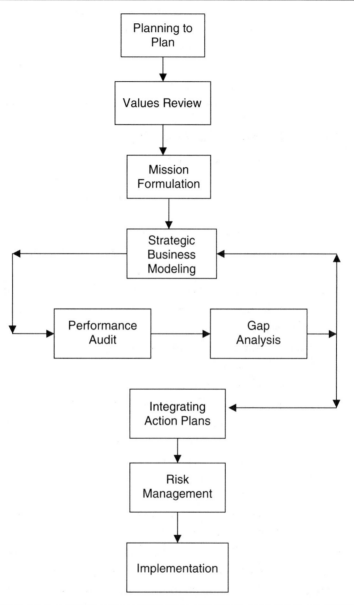

7. **Integrating action plans**: A master business plan must be developed for each line of business, and each organizational unit of the business must develop detailed management control plans and operational control plans based on the overall organizational plan.

8. **Risk management**: Every business is subject to internal and external factors that require contingency planning or risk analysis and planning; the key internal and external risks must be identified, as well as action steps to be taken if the risks arise.

9. **Implementation**: The concurrent initiation of the various management control plans at all levels of the organization and their monitoring by the strategic planning team and upper management.

Enterprise Resource Planning

Enterprise resource planning, or ERP, is an ambitious activity that attempts to integrate all departments and functions across a company onto a single computer system that can serve all those different departments' particular needs. ERP is a logical extension of manufacturing resource planning (MRP) systems, which have been around for years.

ERP combines the operations of many departments into a single, integrated software program that runs off a single database so that the various departments can more easily share information and communicate with each other. In its broadest concept, ERP consists of the following elements:

- Database
- Sales and marketing automation
- Manufacturing execution
- Supply chain management
- Division and corporate financial management
- Human resources
- Corporate management and strategy
- New product development
- Process automation information
- Advanced planning
- Enterprise project management and project management
- Existing MRP II functions.

Typically, ERP automates the back office activities and legacy systems involved in performing the major business processes. Order fulfillment, for example, involves taking an order from a customer, manufacturing the item or taking it from inventory, shipping it, and billing for it. With ERP, when a customer service representative takes an order from a customer, he or she has all the information necessary to complete the order (the customer's credit rating and order history, the company's inventory levels, and the shipping dock's trucking schedule). Everyone else in the company sees the same computer screen and has access to the single database that holds the customer's new order. When one department finishes with the order, the ERP system automatically routes it to the next department. To find out where the order is at any point, one need only log into the ERP system and track it down. Theoretically, the order process moves instantaneously through the organization, and customers get their orders faster and with fewer errors than before. In addition to the business processes listed above, ERP can include project information as discussed below for enterprise project management.

There are three major reasons why companies initially undertake ERP:

1. **To integrate financial data**: As the CEO tries to understand the company's overall performance, he or she may find many different versions of the same data. Finance has one set of revenue numbers, Sales has another version, and the different business units may each have their own versions of how much they contributed to revenues. ERP creates a single version of the data, thus improving communication because everyone is using the same system.

2. **To standardize manufacturing processes**: Manufacturing companies—especially those involved in mergers and acquisitions—often find that multiple business units across the company make the same product using different methods and computer systems. Standardizing those processes and using a single, integrated computer system can save time, increase productivity, and reduce headcount.

3. **To standardize human resources (HR) information**: In companies with multiple business units, HR may not have a unified, simple method for tracking employee time, communicating with employees about benefits and services, and coordinating hiring and layoff practices and timing.

There are several reasons, however, why ERP is growing slowly. The products are currently expensive, and their implementation is complex, which also translates into cost. The third and perhaps major reason is cultural. Moving into a comprehensive ERP requires rethinking the various business processes and their relationship to each other. Many managers have a vested interest in the status quo. Also, top-level strategic and management planning is essential; this requires accountability, something many managers avoid for themselves while insisting on it for others.

ERP, however, is the direction in which the leading-edge companies are moving. It requires planning of the type that affects the selection and scheduling of projects. ERP requires strategic planning—and the communication of the strategic plans to the project managers and other managers of the organization, especially in "management by projects" companies.

In the earlier years of ERP, each application was configured for the client. Therefore, anyone wishing to add another application, such as project management, had to create a custom interface. ERP software modules have been developed to support generic interfaces to high-end project management software.

MANAGEMENT CONTROL PLANNING

There are three sets of major concepts and tools for management control planning and scheduling, as illustrated previously in Figure 2-2:

1. Enterprise-wide project management systems
2. Program management systems
3. Project management systems.

In general, the order reflects the maturity or sophistication of the organization, with the most sophisticated organizations in the process of implementing enterprise-wide management systems based on business strategies and plans.

The first two in this list involve the management of multiple projects. Kerzner points out that using the more sophisticated software packages that are available facilitates the multiple project- and program-wide management planning and scheduling that must be performed. These feature the common database that is necessary for cross-project analysis and reporting. Schedule and cost modules share common files that allow integration among projects and minimize problems of data inconsistencies and redundancies.[6]

Enterprise-Wide Project Management

The more mature organizations view project management principles and practices as key to establishing mechanisms to coordinate, evaluate, and support projects.

Enterprise Project Management

Enterprise project management, EPM, is considered the current state of the art in the management of projects within organizations. It is a subset of ERP focusing on the management of all projects within an organization. EPM usually is implemented in more advanced project management organizations with a central project management office (PMO) leading the way.

EPM capabilities include a focus on accommodating multiple projects across the organization and establishing priorities based on the enterprise strategic plans. More sophisticated project management tools are used. Labor expenditures are tracked by electronic timesheets and cost elements by links to the accounting system.

Resources are planned with a total enterprise perspective using critical chain methodologies or resource leveling across projects. Some organizations use their internal LANs or Internet-based systems to communicate, allowing easy access to the central database used for planning and reporting.

EPM systems require a PMO or equivalent for development, planning, and implementation. The PMO performs the various multiple project analyses needed to balance and allocate resources and to maintain focus on the business strategic objectives. The PMO also manages the day-to-day operation of the EPM system elements.

Portfolio Management

"Portfolio management" is a term used to describe the management process for selecting and establishing priorities between projects by linking to the business strategic plan. It is usually the next step in the organization's maturation process from the single project perspective and is a phase before moving on to implementing EPM fully.

Portfolio management is performed by an organizational entity with the perspective and ability to link project goals to the broader organization goals.

Program Management

In Chapter 1 a program was defined as: "A group of related projects managed in a harmonized way. Programs may include an element of ongoing work until the lifecycle of the program is completed." This definition covers two generic types of multiple-project programs, referred to herein as "lifecycle" programs and "multiple project management" programs.

Multiple projects generally are a group of dependent or independent projects under a single project manager or program manager to use resources efficiently. *Dependent* means that several projects support a program, these projects have links and interactions among them, and the program has a lifecycle. One large project also may be divided into a number of smaller sub-projects, which is also representative of a multiple-project environment. *Independent* means that there is no relationship among the projects except that they share a common resource pool and may represent a program "area."

Lifecycle–Dependent

Lifecycle programs are collections of related projects that correspond to the lifecycle phases: feasibility, planning, implementation, and closeout. These are frequently a series of projects that represent the development and marketing or production and use of a product, especially when one organization has an oversight responsibility or role until the program ends. Examples are the Boeing 777 program, which may have several versions, or a major exhibit in a museum, which may be maintained and updated for several years.

The management goal of lifecycle programs is to maintain consistency and balance as the projects are planned and implemented—moving toward the implementation and operational phases. In lifecycle programs, there is a discrete output from each phase that includes the project plan for the succeeding phase. This concept is described in detail in *Effective Work Breakdown Structures.*[7]

The lifecycle phases for a generic museum exhibit program are illustrated in Figure 2-4. Each phase of the program is planned and implemented as a project, with the program management element providing the overall program planning, direction, and coordination for the several closely related projects. In this situation, there would be an overall program master plan and individual detailed project plans for each phase.

Multiple Project Management—Independent Projects

A program comprising independent projects[8] is perhaps more correctly called a "program area." This would include collections of projects that have a common objective or theme and are under a single program manager or

FIGURE 2-4   Program Structure

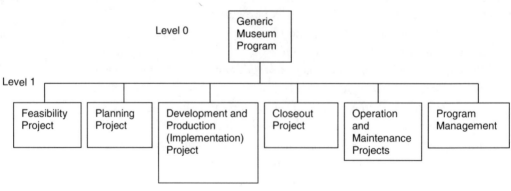

organization manager. Examples are an anti-smoking or measles vaccination program in the Army, an advanced technology program within an organization, or even a television program such as *Sesame Street* or *The Sopranos*. In all these cases, the projects are related to the theme or objective of the program. They may or may not have any lifecycle relationships between them, and the individual projects exist within their own individual lifecycle phases.

Management Challenges

Many difficulties are associated with managing multiple projects. Many project management information systems (PMIS) are oriented toward a single project. Information may be available only on a single project basis. If data are consolidated, often the data collected are inconsistent; therefore, any consolidated reporting may be meaningless. There may be differences in documentation requirements across projects. Interdependencies between projects may not be clear.

The principal challenge, however, is resource allocation. Numerous resource conflicts can occur that lead to other problems. In some organizations, it is difficult to know when planning a project whether or not key resources already have been committed.

There are many differences between managing a large, single project and managing a number of projects. A large single project may have a dedicated team headed by a project manager with specific responsibility and authority to complete the project. A manager of multiple projects typically shares resources with team members working on many projects over a shorter time. Generally, objectives of a single project are clear. Each objective of a project in a multiple-project environment also should be clear, but these objectives may not be consistent across all the projects, particularly if they are carried out for a diverse set of customers. Single projects have definite start and end dates. For the manager of multiple projects, the addition of new projects may necessitate current projects being rescheduled to later dates, and changes in scope and priorities may be required. Single projects are more independent, while multiple projects typically are integrated.

Some key management issues in a multiple project environment are:
- How will the project manager control the projects?
- What are the interdependencies among projects?
- Who will provide information to whom?
- How often are data needed?
- Are there different goals at the program vs. the project level?

Organizations need the ability to provide workload planning and resource allocation to ensure effective and efficient use of resources.

Standardization

A standard project management methodology that is used across the organization is necessary in a multiple-project management environment. It supports improved resource management by using a structured approach to planning and implementation that enables staff and other resources to be used when needed, reducing the frequency of unexpected downtime or overloaded resource commitments. More attention is directed to risks throughout the lifecycle, providing a greater potential to identify opportunities and respond to threats. With a consistent methodology, there is a common frame of reference for project evaluation and a common use of terms to facilitate communication.

Project performance data, or metrics, can be collected for an organization-wide measurement program to monitor each ongoing project and to provide information for future project selection, planning, and execution decisions.

Standard tools also are needed to facilitate managing multiple projects. These include standard software for project management, risk management, word processing, spreadsheets, and presentations, as well as a standard e-mail system.

A standardized coding system should be adopted across projects for:
- Work breakdown structures
- Resources
- Task names
- Calendars.

Standard coding facilitates consistent reporting by project managers and linking multiple projects in a single PMIS. Standard processes, such as a standard change control system, standard meeting schedules, standard report formats, project review formats, and reporting frequency, are necessary.

Scheduling and Resource Allocation

The key to managing multiple projects is the ability to allocate resources across projects, especially key personnel, and to be able to set priorities among projects.

In scheduling and resource allocation, two approaches can be used: (1) treating multiple projects as if they were one large project, or (2) considering each project independently. Each approach leads to different outcomes.

There are two key considerations:

1. Slippage on one project may begin a ripple effect, causing other projects to slip. Expediting one project to prevent slippage also can have a boomerang effect.
2. Projects in a multiple project environment compete for the same scarce resources.

Success depends on how effectively resources are used. Resource allocation is difficult because there may not be:

- A formal organization-wide resource allocation process
- Adequate visibility of resource over-commitment
- An organization-wide master plan for all projects
- Leadership resolve.

Enough resources to support all projects are seldom available. Often this situation is ignored, and the organization tries to pursue too many projects at once. Because of resource constraints in multiple project management, network planning, critical chain, resource leveling, and other resource planning and control methodologies are used. These need to be applied above the individual projects at the program level. (These are touched on briefly below and discussed in more detail in later sections.)

While network planning is not a resource allocation method *per se*, it can be used to assess tradeoffs between time and other resources. Each project can be "crashed," that is, the total project duration can be decreased after a number of alternatives are analyzed to determine how to obtain the maximum duration compression for the least cost. The focus is on crashing time, not on resource use or availability.

A variation of network planning is using "critical chain" techniques that focus specifically and explicitly on critical resources and resource management.

Resource loading analyses and histograms show the individual resources a project requires at specific time periods. They show the total resource requirements and provide the first step to reducing excessive demands on some resources.

Leveling addresses whether resources are over-used or under-used. It should be considered on an activity-by-activity basis, as project staff members typically are not interchangeable. When resource loadings are leveled, the associated costs also will be leveled. It often is less expensive to level labor resources to avoid the need for layoffs or new hires.

How multiple projects are sequenced has a bearing on the overall performance of projects in a program. If the projects are interrelated, considerable planning is needed to identify the start and finish dates of each project. If these dates are not carefully chosen, scheduling bottlenecks may arise, and overall program performance may deteriorate.

Planning and scheduling multiple projects usually involves some sort of multi-project scheduling algorithm and should be considered part of a portfolio, as described. These activities are doubly resource-constrained in the sense that there is usually a total program budget within which the program manager or department manager must operate. In addition, key persons are needed to support several projects, and their availability affects the plans and schedules of the individual projects.

Project Management

Project-level tools used for planning and scheduling include:
1. Project charter
2. Gantt charts
3. Milestone charts
4. Network planning
5. Project plans.

Chapter 3 contains a detailed description of the project planning and scheduling process.

Project Charter

The project charter is the primary document used to define a project and to establish the general framework for its implementation. A commonly used variant, the project manager's charter, serves as a contract between the project manager and the project sponsor and establishes the parameters of the project manager's responsibility and authority. This includes a description of assigned resources. It usually is issued following an authorization to spend resources on a project and may include a statement of work.

The project manager should prepare this document, which then is reviewed and approved by senior management and, in some cases, the customer. In some organizations, the PM is assigned after the charter is completed. The charter is an essential planning and communication tool when projects are managed within a matrix organization environment. Here it is essential for the supporting organizations to concur with the charter. Formal sign-offs are recommended.

Project charters vary in size and comprehensiveness depending on the size and complexity of the project. They usually are from three to ten pages in length. For small projects, the project charter may be a verbal agreement with a supervisor or other sponsor; however, the project manager should document the agreement for his or her own reference. (Managers are known for their poor memories, especially when problems arise.)

Paragraphs and sections within a project charter may vary from project to project, but the major areas to be addressed are shown in Figure 2-5.

The project charter outline should be tailored to the project and the project environment. Only partial information may be available in the feasibility phase, and the charter should be updated as information is developed. The charter should include all the information and guidance needed to add resources and to begin project planning.

Gantt Charts

A Gantt chart is a graphic representation of the activities in a project arrayed in chronological order on a time scale, with bars representing activity duration. It was developed as a production control tool before World War II

FIGURE 2-5   Project Charter Outline

PROJECT CHARTER OUTLINE

Project Purpose
Project Objectives
Summary Project Description
   *General Description of the Work
   *Description of the End Product and Expected Quality
     or Performance
   *Schedule and Budget
   *Resources to be Provided
Project Manager
   *Authority
   *Responsibility
   *Coordination Requirements
   *Reporting Requirements
Facilities and Environment
Supporting Activities/Organizations
   *Resources to be Supplied
Customer and Customer Relationship Management
Transfer or Delivery of the End Product

---

by Henry L. Gantt, an American engineer and social scientist, and is used to show the major activities of a project and its key events or milestones. Gantt charts are easy to construct. They may be simple versions created on graph paper or more complex automated versions created using project management software. The Gantt chart format is the primary display used in many project management software applications.

Before the advent of the current planning techniques, companies used professional planners and schedulers to prepare the Gantt charts used for managing large projects. These individuals understood the order in which activities needed to be accomplished, the relationships between the activities, and the historic durations of the activities. In the 1940s, 1950s, and later, teams of schedulers would prepare the project schedules for complex items, such as developing new aircraft, ships, or hydroelectric dams. These Gantt charts would contain thousands of activities and were prepared manually.

A Gantt chart is constructed with a horizontal axis representing the total time span of the project, subdivided into increments (for example, days, weeks, or months), and a vertical axis containing a list of the activities that make up the project. The list was placed in chronological order, and the Gantt charts were sometimes called "waterfall charts."

Figure 2-6 shows a Gantt chart for the initial production of an aircraft external fuel tank pylon.

Horizontal bars of varying lengths represent the time span for each activity. The bar spans may overlap, indicating that different activities are to be performed during the same time span. The bars are often shown initially as open rectangles. As the project progresses, secondary bars, arrowheads, or darkened bars may be added to indicate completed activities or the portions of activities that have been completed. A vertical line is often used to represent the current reporting date. Various symbols are used to show dates, relationships, and important events. It is useful to create separate Gantt charts for individual areas of responsibility.

Automated Gantt charts store more information about activities, such as the individuals assigned to specific activities, and any notes. They also offer the benefits of being easy to understand and to change.

Gantt charts give a clear illustration of project status. Their major drawback is that they do not show activity dependencies—it is not possible to tell how one activity falling behind schedule affects other activities. Percentage completion data, if shown, also need an explanation regarding whether the reference is to performance, schedule, or cost. Also, they are not suitable for what-if studies or modeling of the project plan.

FIGURE 2-6   Gantt Chart

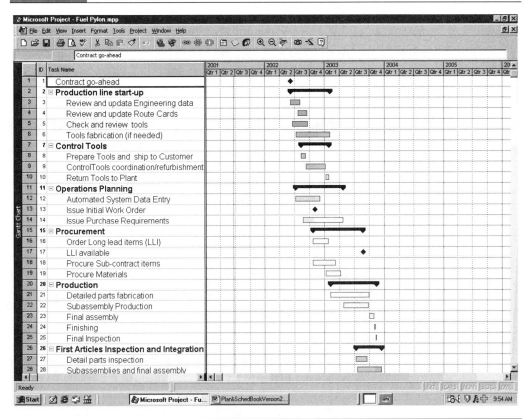

Gantt *displays*, however, are the preferred choice for presenting schedule data. Their shortcomings are readily corrected by using project management software to develop the information and presenting the output from this software in Gantt chart format.

Milestone Charts

Throughout the life of a project—from establishing the project to closeout—many events occur. The most significant events are designated as "milestones." These milestones are used to measure the progress achieved on a project and the performance of those responsible for controlling the project. Progress payments are often based on the verified attainment of key milestones.

It is recommended that each significant internal or external deliverable or completion of a significant activity be shown as a milestone on the Gantt chart. This should be done regardless of the planning method used. The activity bar should be terminated with a milestone, as shown in Figure 2-7. Each milestone needs an unambiguous descriptor that includes the word "start" or "complete" or the equivalent. When using project management software, a milestone is a zero duration activity, indicated graphically on the screen or when printed by a triangle or diamond. This makes the Gantt chart significantly easier to use and focuses attention on major events.

Intermediate milestones also must be met during the project. These milestones are defined by the project manager and can be shown on the Gantt chart. Important meetings and reviews are often shown as milestones, especially when they are the culmination of several predecessor activities.

Figure 2-8 depicts a pure milestone chart with the summary work area elements shown as lines with milestones at the ends. Except where indicated as "start" on the activity description, each milestone is assumed to be the completion of the activity. Also, "start" events usually begin at the start of the day on which they are scheduled, and milestones or "complete" events usually end at the end of the work day.

Sometimes a simple tabular listing is the easiest way to present a schedule. A sample is shown in Figure 2-9.

Network Planning

The advent of network planning in 1957 represented the most significant improvement in project planning and scheduling since the Gantt chart was invented 50 years earlier. It also signaled the beginning of project management as a profession because a formal body of knowledge started to evolve at that time.

This chapter will continue to describe the various project planning and scheduling tools. Chapter 3 will describe in much more detail how to develop network diagrams and the more sophisticated aspects of their development.

Network planning is deceptively simple. In its simplest form, the activities that might be displayed in a Gantt chart are arrayed and lines are drawn between them to show their relationships graphically. For example, assume that a dinner party is to be planned, and the first three activities are to prepare

---

FIGURE 2-7   Milestone Terminating a Key Activity

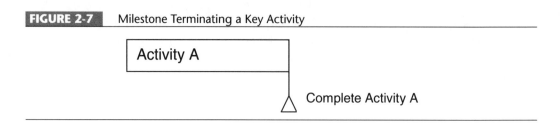

FIGURE 2-8   Milestone Chart

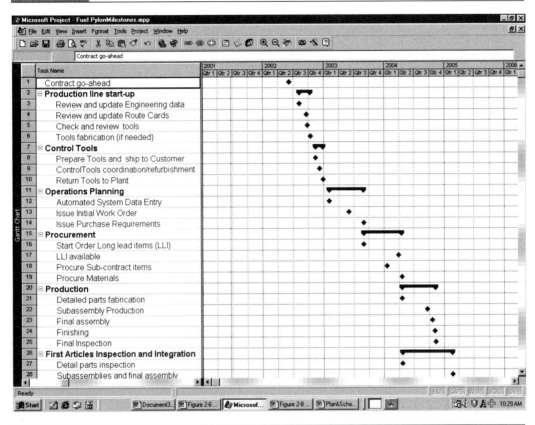

a shopping list, shop for drinks, and shop for food. In a Gantt chart, these would be three simple bars. In network planning, these would be shown as displayed in Figure 2-10.

In network planning, the length of the bars identifying the activities has no significance; the time durations are written on the bars or entered into a computer program. What is significant is the relationship between the activities, which is identified by the arrows. The interpretation of Figure 2-10 is that neither shopping for drinks nor shopping for food can start until the activity "Make Shopping List" is completed. Using this type of logic, the entire list of project activities may be represented in network format.

The term "network planning" includes three basic types of network diagrams: the Program Evaluation and Review Technique (PERT), the Critical Path Method (CPM), and the Precedence Diagramming Method (PDM). Their characteristics are compared in Figure 2-11.

FIGURE 2-9   Tabular Listing

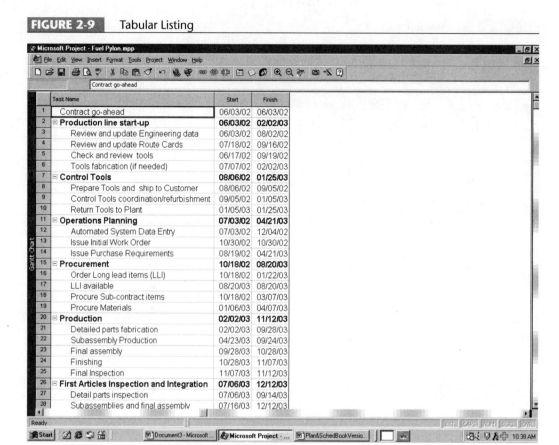

CPM and PERT are discussed first to provide historical perspective and describe their contributions to today's project management body of knowledge. Both CPM and PERT were developed independently at about the same. CPM, or the Critical Path Method, was developed in 1957 by Morgan R. Walker of the Engineering Services Division of the Du Pont

FIGURE 2-10   Network Planning

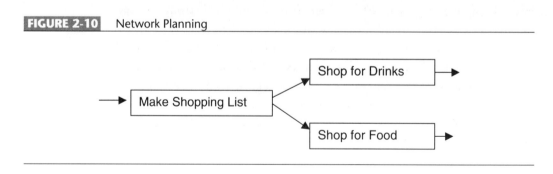

FIGURE 2-11   Types of Network Diagrams

TYPES OF NETWORK DIAGRAMS			
Characteristics	Types		
Generic	1. Activity-on-Arrow		2. Activity-on-Node
Names and Acronyms	A. Program Evaluation and Review Technique (PERT)	B. Arrow Diagramming Method (ADM) or Critical Path Method (CPM)	Precedence Diagramming Method (PDM)
Time Estimates	3 per Activity	1 per Activity	1 per Activity
Milestone Terminology	Events	Milestones	Zero duration activity
Activity Terminology	Activities and Dummy Activities	Activities	Activities
Graphics	Events are circles, activities are lines with arrows	Activities are lines with arrows, events are small circles or nodes	Activities are rectangles and milestones are triangles

Company and by James E. Kelley, who was at that time with the Remington Rand Company. Walker and Kelly were concerned with the problem of improving scheduling techniques for the Du Pont Company's Refinery Renovation Project and such other projects as the building of a pilot model plant and the shutdown of a plant for overhaul and maintenance.[9] Recognizing that all activities of such projects must be executed in a well-defined sequence, they came up with the arrow diagram as the most logical representation of the interrelationships between jobs for any project. Their method of calculating the longest or critical path through the arrow diagram or network is the same algorithm used for the PERT network and PERT critical path calculation.

Kelley and Walker used a single-time estimate for the duration of each activity and did not go into the problem of uncertainty of time duration for individual jobs. Because CPM and PERT were independent developments, the notations of the systems are quite different, as can be seen in Figure 2-12. PDM is included to have a complete set. The PDM notation tends to follow CPM.

During the period of the early development of the CPM networking technique, Kelley,[10] Fulkerson,[11] and Clark[12] did most of the underlying mathematical work, and their referenced papers are basic in this field.

Network Planning Notation

PERT versus CPM versus PDM Notation		
PERT	CPM	PDM
Network	Arrow Diagram	Network
Event	Node	Milestone
Activity	Job	Activity
Activity Expected Time t_e, calculated based on three time estimates (lower case)	Activity Duration Single Time Estimate	Activity Duration Single Time Estimate
Slack (primary)	Total Float	Total Float
Slack (secondary)	Free Float	Free Float
Event T_E, T_L Earliest or Expected Time and Latest Time (upper case)	Activity Earliest Start, Earliest Finish, ES & EF	Activity Earliest Start, Earliest Finish, ES & EF
Event T_E, T_L	Activity Latest Start, Latest Finish, LS & LF	Activity Latest Start, Latest Finish, LS & LF

PERT was developed in the Navy's Special Projects Office because of the recognition of Admiral W. F. Raborn that something better was needed in the form of an integrated planning and control system for the Fleet Ballistic Missile (FBM) program, commonly known as the Polaris Weapons System. Based on his support, a research team was established in 1958 to work on a project designated as Program Evaluation Research Task, or PERT. By the time of the first internal Navy report on the subject, PERT had become "Program Evaluation and Review Technique," and thus it has persisted until this day, when it has become part of the everyday language of industry.

D. G. Malcolm, J. H. Roseboom, C. E. Clark, and W. Fazar, all of the original Navy-sponsored research team, were the authors of the first publicly published paper on PERT, which was included in the September 1959 issue of *Operations Research*.[13] Because of the complexity and size of the Polaris program, this original research team decided to restrict the initial application of PERT to the time area, although it was expanded later to PERT Cost.

There are two significant differences between PERT and CPM or PDM. The first is that PERT focuses on events or milestones that represent the start and completion of activities, while the other networking techniques focus on the work performed or the activities themselves. The second difference is that PERT uses three time estimates for each activity and a formula to determine the expected duration of each activity. Because of the probabilistic nature of the estimates, it is also possible to make statistical statements about the probability of meeting any specific target completion date. This is discussed in more detail in Chapter 4.

Since the time of these original contributions to the development and application of the network technique, the amount of literature on CPM and PERT, and the number of management systems derived from them, have been enormous.

These three types of network diagrams are illustrated in Figure 2-13 using the same basic dinner party plan. The network diagrams are for the identical project, but note the significant differences in the graphics.

PERT Networks—The PERT network focuses on the start and completion of events that are associated with each activity. This is what the Navy was interested in when the technique was developed: When does each activity start, and when is it completed? Has it started or has it been completed? What events must occur before an activity can start? What events are constrained by the completion of other activities?

While used for planning, the emphasis was also on reporting. It was an invaluable discipline to put down on paper what formerly was in the heads of experienced schedulers—except that no scheduler had experience in the complexities of a Fleet Ballistic Missile Program, so teams from various organizations collaborated in developing the networks.

There are two types of arrows in the PERT diagram. The normal activity, where the work is performed, is always bounded by two events—a starting event and a completing event. The other arrows are called "dummy activities" because they represent no work, and their role is to identify the relationships between events.

When developing a PERT network, it was frequently convenient to start at the end of the project and constantly ask, while working backward, what activities or events must occur immediately before this event or activity can occur? Alternatively, a list of activities would be prepared and the related events identified and linked in their logical order by dummy activities.

A larger number of symbols (circles and arrows) is required to develop the PERT network as compared to the CPM or PDM networks. The biggest problem with the graphics was the transition to the use of project management software on personal computers. Software developers used the Gantt chart as the basic format for display and to identify predecessor/successor relationships. As a result, PDM has become the de facto standard.

Another problem with PERT was the three time estimates required for each activity, which added complexity and additional work to the process.

FIGURE 2-13   Network Diagrams

PERT DIAGRAM

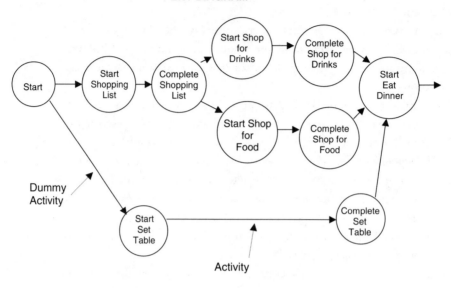

ACTIVITY-ON-ARROW DIAGRAM (CPM)

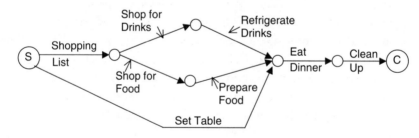

PDM DIAGRAM

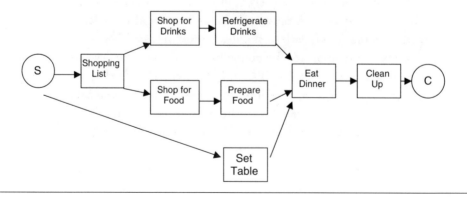

Many persons questioned the validity of the results because of the GIGO predisposition (garbage-in, garbage-out). However, current concepts of risk analysis have revisited the three-time estimate concept and have adopted its features.

Activity-on-Arrow (CPM) Networks—The CPM networks are also activity-on-arrow networks like PERT; the emphasis, however, is on the work being performed and the relationships between the activities. The nodes are needed only to identify activities numerically. This was for the convenience of the early project software programs that required a specific numbering system referred to as "i – j." The number of the node at the beginning of an activity had to be a smaller number than the node at the end. The graphics are very efficient and easy to read and understand. They are still used in construction projects and are drawn easily by a draftsman-planner. Blueprints are made and distributed to the job.

PDM Networks—As mentioned, the network format scheme of choice is PDM. It is the scheme used by most project management software programs. It lends itself to readily understandable translation to Gantt chart format for display because the activity boxes represent the Gantt bars. The default screen display is normally in Gantt chart format, and the constraints between activities are easily identified.

A sample of a PDM network, for the project illustrated in Gantt chart form earlier, is shown in Figure 2-14. The display is from Microsoft Project 98® and is referred to by the software developer as the "PERT view."

Figure 2-15 illustrates the events and activities on the network diagram in more detail. The name, ID number, duration, start date, and completion date are included for each activity. In addition, summary activities from the WBS are shown with similar detail. For example, included in the figure "Production Line Start-up" is a summary activity or work package. (See Figure 2-6 for the comparable Gantt chart view.)

Network planning is the most important tool to ensure the schedule logic because it identifies relationships and interdependencies among activities. Chapter 3 discusses other advantages, including the ability to identify the critical activities in the schedule and the ability to be used for "what if" studies.

The disadvantage associated with network charts in the PDM, PERT, or CPM formats is that they can become very large, complex, and difficult to display in hard copy. Figure 2-14 illustrates this problem for a very small project. With the current project management software, the constraints are identified within the computer, and the Gantt format is used for display; the

FIGURE 2-14 Project Network Diagram

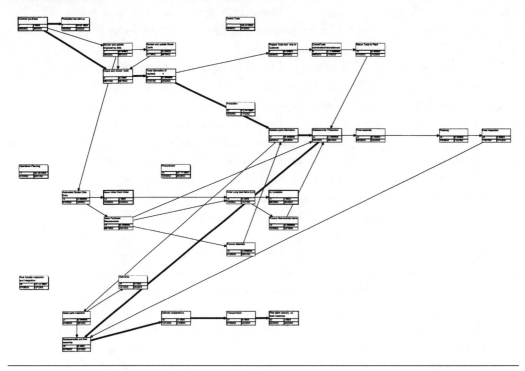

linkages are displayed or hidden at the choice of the user. Also, as will be seen in Chapter 3, network development is more complex than a simple Gantt chart, and some experience or training is needed to become proficient.

In summary, network charts are an important discipline to depict the logic and interdependencies among the project activities and force careful planning by all involved with the project.

Concepts of Critical Path and Float (Slack)—Network planning provides more information than is available from simply preparing a Gantt chart. The nature of the technique allows for two very important concepts: critical path and float (or slack). Regardless of the format of the network, the longest path through the network is called the "critical path" because any slippage in any activity on the longest path will cause the end date of the project to slip a like amount.

When using management by exception, it is clear that focus must be on the activities on the critical path to make sure they do not slip. To reduce the length of time planned for the total project, the duration of activities on the critical path needs to be reduced or the plan changed. As you reduce the

FIGURE 2-15   Project Network Diagram Detail

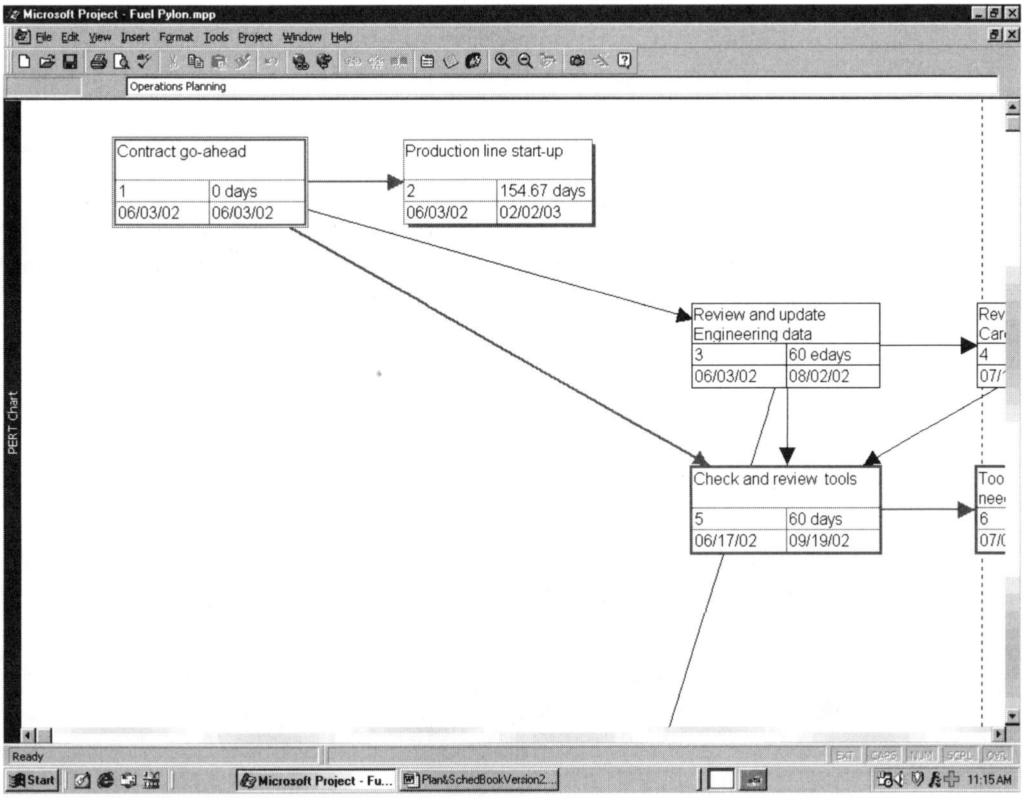

duration of activities on the critical path, other paths may become critical as well. Similarly, during project execution, delays in activities on paths other than the critical path may result in the other paths becoming critical.

"Total slack or total float" refers to the amount of slack on the path where the particular activity is located. The "0" slack activities are on the critical path, and other values of slack indicate the amount of working time an activity on the path could be delayed before becoming critical. Non-critical paths may be adjusted or replanned to the extent that slack or float exists without affecting the project completion date.

Often, the schedule must be changed to meet constraints. Both schedule duration and resource allocations must be considered. Attack the critical path first. Consider the following options:

- Reduce activity durations by taking a closer look at the estimates to reduce contingency.
- Adjust activity durations by considering probabilities, i.e., accept more schedule risk.
- Change the plan by altering precedence relationships, where feasible.
- In any event, compress earlier activities first to leave later options open.

"Free slack or free float" refers to the amount of slack any *individual* activity has and represents the amount it can move or float without affecting the start of any succeeding activity.

The amount of slack that exists becomes important in adjusting the plan for resource conflicts. It is common when planning projects and assigning or estimating resources for each activity that certain persons are required for more than 100 percent of their time in a particular time period. This occurs most often when multiple projects are being managed simultaneously in an organization. If float is available, it can be used to adjust the timing of activities to resolve these problems.

Examples of the calculations of the critical path and slack are included in Chapter 3.

Graphical Evaluation and Review Technique (GERT)—GERT is a network analysis methodology that allows for non-sequential activities, such as loops (e.g., a test that must be repeated more than once) or conditional branches (e.g., a design update that is needed only if the inspection detects errors). These options are useful in certain situations because the other networking techniques do not allow loops or conditional branches. GERT combines signal flowchart theory, probabilistic networks, PERT, and decision trees all in a single framework.[14]

Instead of a network consisting of events and activities or nodes and arrows, as in the case of PERT and PDM, a network consists of logical nodes and directed arcs. Two parameters are provided—one being the probability that a given arc is taken and the second being the distribution function describing the time required by the activity.

The computer evaluation of the network results in the probability of each node being realized and the probable elapsed time between all nodes.

Figure 2-16, adapted from Meredith and Mantel, presents the difference between GERT and PERT/CPM.[15]

GERT is most useful as a computer simulation that provides a probabilistic analysis of the system being modeled: a research and development (R&D) project, a production process, or a process with decision points

FIGURE 2-16   Comparison of GERT and PERT/CPM

GERT	PERT/CPM
Branching from a node is probabilistic	Branching from a node is deterministic
Various possible probability distributions for time estimates	A formula approximating the shape of the beta probability distribution is used for time estimates
Flexibility in node realization	No flexibility in node realization
Looping back to earlier events is acceptable	Looping back is not allowed
Difficult to use as a control tool	Easy to use as a control tool
Arcs may represent time, cost, reliability, etc.	Arcs represent time only

and feedback. Figure 2-17 illustrates a GERT network using some of the technique's unique symbols.

Critical Chain Project Management—In 1997 Dr. Eliyahu M. Goldratt published a book titled *Critical Chain* that presents a different approach to project planning and scheduling.[16] Critical Chain Project Management (CCPM) claims to improve project planning by ensuring that it is immune from reasonable uncertainty or statistical fluctuations, referred to as common cause variation. It does this by establishing time buffers at the ends of network activity paths rather than building them into each activity. Three types of buffers are used—the project buffer protects the overall project completion on the critical chain path, feeding buffers protect the critical chain from merging path delays, and resource buffers help make sure key resources are

FIGURE 2-17   Sample GERT Diagram

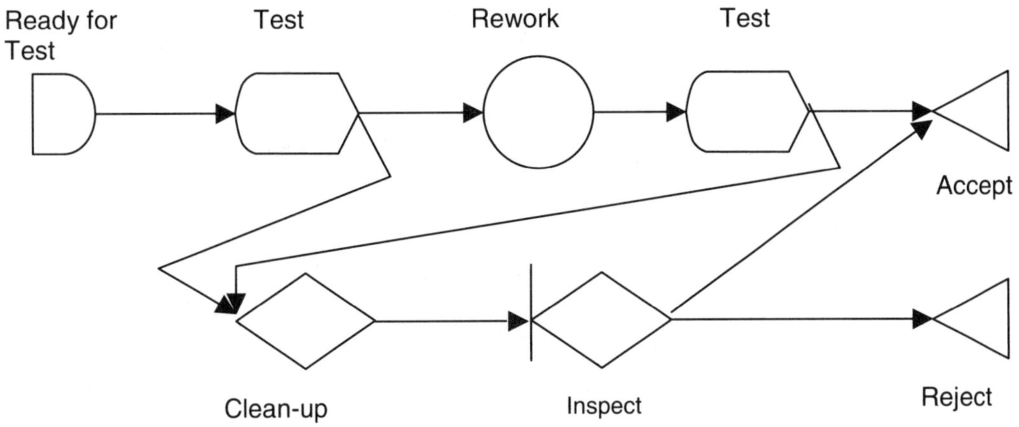

35

available when needed. Figure 2-18 illustrates the use of buffers in a simple PDM network.

Buffer management enhances measurement and decision making for project control. According to the adherents of CCPM, projects using the methodology have a greatly improved record of schedule, cost, and scope performance. CCPM has some unique features that separate it from the general planning and scheduling methodology outlined in this book and the *PMBOK® Guide*. These include the following five features, which are adapted from Leach:[17]

1. CCPM uses the term "critical chain" rather than the term "critical path" as the series of activities that determines the total project duration. In CCPM the critical chain includes resource constraints as well as activity time constraints. The activities that comprise the critical chain remain fixed during project implementation and do not change.

2. Activity duration estimating is based on 50 percent probability rather than the more customary 90 percent figure (see Chapter 3). CCPM aggregates allowances for the uncertainty of the estimates into buffers at the end of activity chains.

3. Monitoring the buffers provides the primary metrics used to determine when corrective action is necessary to control the project schedule.

4. Multiple project management is performed by first identifying the company key constraining resource. All projects are linked through this resource and use buffers to account for activity duration variability.

FIGURE 2-18   Critical Chain Project and Feeding Buffers

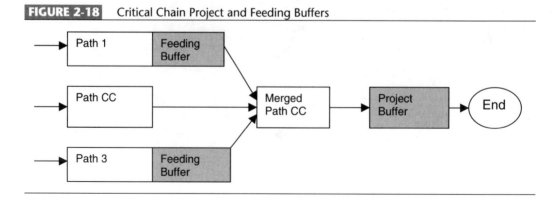

5. Project team behavior and organization culture is changed to encourage early completion and reporting of activities, focusing on the work and not a schedule date. Multitasking by individuals is eliminated.

Chapter 4 discusses additional details of implementing CCPM.

Project Plans

The project plan is developed during the planning phase of a project and provides the basis for implementation. Approval of the project plan signals the end of the planning phase. The project plan usually contains at least the following sections:

- Project charter
- Work breakdown structure
- Description of the scope of the project or the statement of work
- Description of the deliverables and when and how they are to be delivered and accepted
- Description of the resources assigned to the project and the organization
- Master schedule
- Description of the risks and plans for mitigation of the major risks
- Methodology for change management.

A more complete description of the project plan and the recommended contents of each part are included in Chapter 3.

OPERATIONAL CONTROL PLANNING

Operational planning and control is the process of ensuring that specific activities are carried out effectively and efficiently. Operational planning techniques are deterministic, that is, the durations of the activities are established by the nature of the process. Once the planning is complete, little judgment is required regarding what is to be done and how long it will take. The focus is on execution and maintaining the process within control boundaries. The following operational control scheduling tools have features related to network planning.

Material Resource Planning

This is sometimes called Material Requirements Planning or Manufacturing Requirements Planning. MRP is the common term for an automated system for establishing and communicating the schedules for all manufacturing process activities necessary to meet the delivery requirements established by the contract with the customer. Only a summary overview is provided because MRP is used for production planning and scheduling and generally not for project planning and scheduling. Project managers should understand the principles of MRP because project deliverables frequently become production items, leading to a phase-in to MRP.

Figure 2-19 illustrates the operation of a typical MRP system. Selected major components are:

Bills of material—maintains the product structure information for the materials, resources, tools, and other items needed for manufacturing the products in the factory. The bills of material function identifies the materials required for each product at each workstation in terms of items needed from predecessor work stations, raw materials, and purchased items from inventory. The actual bill of material is a product work breakdown structure to the detail of every part, nut, and bolt going into the end item.

MRP planning and scheduling—calculates and maintains an optimum material plan based on the master production schedule, inventory status, and bills of material. This component generates the detailed schedules for each item at each work station when new orders are received. It adjusts schedules when shortages occur and is the heart of the system.

FIGURE 2-19 Material Resource Planning System

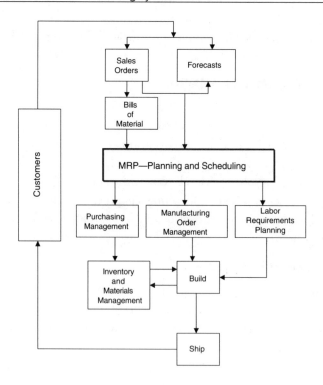

Purchasing management—the preparation, release, and status of purchase orders based on the bill of material, the master schedule of deliveries, procurement lead times, quantity, and shop need times. Information is provided to buyers or the supply chain management system.

Inventory management—maintenance of data on inventory requirements, balances, and stock locations.

Manufacturing order management—the preparation and release of manufacturing orders based on manufacturing workstation setup, the master schedule of deliveries, work station manufacturing process flow times, quantity requirements, and inventory availability. In addition, quantities to draw from inventory to support the manufacturing orders for each workstation are identified.

Line of Balance

The Line of Balance technique (LOB) was conceived approximately 65 years ago to provide management with visibility on production or recurring activities. The U.S. Navy in World War II (1942–1943) developed LOB and published a brochure in 1958 that described the technique in detail and recommended its use for production surveillance.[18] Iannone describes the concept as follows:[19]

> Line of Balance is a technique for assembling, selecting, interpreting, and presenting in graphic form the essential factors involved in a production process from raw materials to completion of the end product, against a background of time. It is essentially a management-type tool, utilizing the principle of exception to show only the most important facts to its audience. It is a means of integrating the flow of materials and components into manufacture of end items in accordance with phased delivery requirements.

LOB relies on graphic displays, as illustrated in color in the Navy document[20] in Figure 2-20.

Four elements make up the LOB technique. The LOB display chart has three distinctive sections, as seen on the figure: the objective, the progress chart, and the production plan. The fourth part is the line of balance itself, as displayed on the progress chart. The line of balance is generated graphically using manual techniques or computer software to reflect the required production status at a particular point in time. Each of the four parts is reviewed below in more detail:

Objective Display—The first element of the LOB chart is the objective section, which is displayed in the upper left corner of the figure. In produc-

FIGURE 2-20 Line of Balance Display

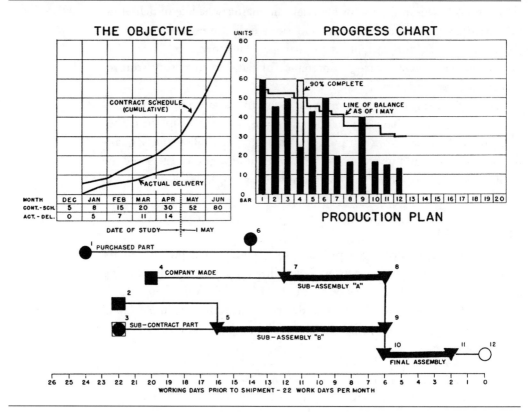

tion, the objective is to manufacture units for delivery; in the illustration, 80 units are to be delivered. The display presents cumulative planned delivery by month, versus cumulative actual delivery. At the time of this display (30 April) 30 units should have been delivered, but only 14 deliveries had actually been made. As will be seen, it is important that the contract schedule curve be plotted accurately.

Production Plan—The second element of LOB is the production plan, shown across the bottom of the figure. The production process is presented as a "set-back" chart on a time scale. The set-back chart is drawn working back from the point of delivery as shown. In the figure, delivery is identified as control point 12. The production of each article is shown to occur over a 25-day working sequence, starting with the first control point or event. To make the chart easier to read, special symbols and heavy lines are used customarily for assembly activities. The specific work to be performed is often written on the activity line in the setback chart, as shown on the production plan.

Progress Chart—The third element of LOB, the progress chart, is shown in the upper right side of the figure. The progress chart displays the 80 units to be delivered on the vertical scale and lists the components of the production plan, specified by number, across the bottom. Both the objective chart and the progress chart use the same scale. As individual components are completed or procured components become available, the quantities of each are indicated in a barometer-like vertical display on this chart.

Line of Balance—The fourth element is the generation of the line of balance as of a particular date. The line is established by using the number of setback days for each component and graphically developing the line using the contract schedule curve. Using control point 5—the start of subassembly "B"—as an example, it must be completed 16 days prior to delivery. Starting from the intersection of the status date, 30 April, and the cumulative contract schedule curve on the objective chart, a horizontal line representing 16 days' duration is drawn on the objective chart. Next, the point at the end of the line is projected upward to intersect with the delivery schedule curve. This identifies the number of units of control point 5 that should be completed, taking into account its setback times. This point is projected horizontally over the bar labeled "5" on the progress chart, and a heavy line is drawn. Figure 2-21 illustrates this process.

FIGURE 2-21   Drawing the Line of Balance

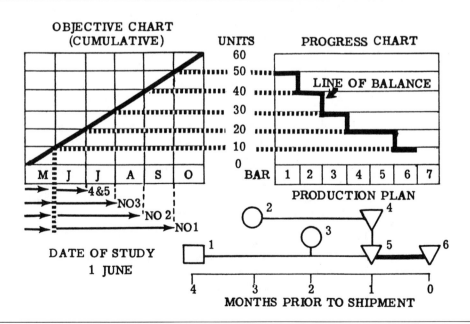

This process is repeated for each of the 12 control points, and the ends of the horizontal lines on the progress chart are connected to become the line of balance. The status of each item then is clearly displayed, and it is obvious that the items to be produced at control points 2 and 3 are currently delaying the production.

This is a very simple example; in practice, the deliverable items are much more complex.

NOTES

1. Robert N. Anthony, *Planning and Control Systems: A Framework for Analysis* (Boston: Harvard University Graduate School of Business Administration, 1965), p. 1.
2. Ibid., p. 16.
3. Ibid, p. 17.
4. Ibid.
5. Leonard Goodstein, Timothy Nolan, and J. William Pfeiffer, *Applied Strategic Planning: A Comprehensive Guide* (San Diego: Pfeiffer & Co., 1992).
6. Harold Kerzner, *Project Management: A Systems Approach to Planning, Scheduling, and Controlling*, 7th edition (New York: John Wiley & Sons, 2001), p. 707.
7. Gregory T. Haugan, *Effective Work Breakdown Structures* (Vienna, VA: Management Concepts, Inc., 2002).
8. The material in this section on multiple project management is adapted from the Management Concepts, Inc., training course of the same name.
9. Associated General Contractors, *CPM in Construction: A Manual for General Contractors* (Washington, D.C.: Associated General Contractors, 1965), p. 9.
10. J. Kelley, "Critical Path Planning and Scheduling: Mathematical Basis," *Operations Research* 1961; 9(3): 296–321.
11. D. Fulkerson, "A Network Flow Computation for Project Cost Curves." *Management Sciences* 1961; 7: 167–178.
12. C. Clark, "The Optimum Allocation of Resources Among Activities of a Network," *Journal of Industrial Engineering* 1961; 12(January-February): 11–17.
13. D.G. Malcolm, J.H. Roseboom, C.E. Clark, and W. Fazar, "Application of a Technique for Research and Development Program Evaluation," *Operations Research* 1959; 7(5): 646–670.
14. Jack R. Meredith and Samuel J. Mantel, Jr., *Project Management: A Managerial Approach*, 3rd edition (New York: John Wiley & Sons, 1995), p. 364.
15. Ibid.
16. Eliyahu M. Goldratt, *Critical Chain* (Great Barrington, MA: The North River Press Publishing Corporation, 1997).
17. Lawrence P. Leach, "Critical Chain Project Management Improves Project Performance," *Project Management Journal*, June 1999, p. 39.
18. Office of Naval Material Line of Balance Technology (Department of the Navy: NAVEXOS P 1851, 24 February 1958).
19. Anthony L. Iannone, *Management Program Planning and Control with PERT, MOST and LOB* (Englewood Cliffs, NJ: Prentice-Hall, Inc., 1967), p. 129.
20. Office of Naval Material Line of Balance Technology (Department of the Navy: NAVEXOS P 1851, 24 February 1958), p. vi.

CHAPTER 3

Steps in Project Planning and Scheduling

Chapter 2 presented the many planning and scheduling tools that are available to project managers. This chapter focuses on the specific steps to be taken to develop a plan and schedule for a project. Various aspects of the different techniques discussed in Chapter 2 are used in these steps.

Figure 3-1 presents the seven steps necessary to develop an effective schedule for a project. Each block is a subsection of this chapter. The process is straightforward and applies to all projects. It doesn't matter whether the project is a multimillion dollar activity involving thousands of people or very small, involving a few people in an office—the steps are the same. Steps 1 and 2 are where the activities to be performed get defined. Step 3 is the preparation of the network diagram using these activities. Steps 4 and 5 include the estimation of the duration of each activity and the estimation of the resource requirements. From these data the schedule can be developed, with specific dates for each activity start and finish, and the baseline for implementing the project and for control can be established.

STEP 1: ESTABLISHING THE PLANNING FRAMEWORK— THE WBS

The work breakdown structure (WBS) is the key tool in the planning phase to assist in work definition and to provide the framework for the plans and schedules. The interaction of the WBS and plans and schedules is described in a Department of Defense (DOD) document as follows:[1]

Planning work by WBS elements serves as the basis for estimating and scheduling resource requirements. The work breakdown structure assists in managing cost, schedule, and technical performance. By breaking the total product into successively smaller entities, management can ensure that all required products are identified in terms of cost, schedule, and performance goals. Assigning performance budgets to work segments and identifying responsible units produces a time-phased plan against which

FIGURE 3-1   Project Planning and Scheduling Process

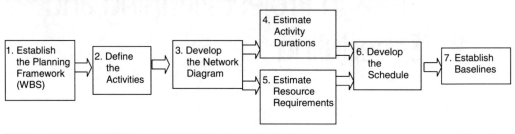

actual performance can be measured. Corrective action can be taken when deviations from the plan are identified. This integrated approach to work planning also simplifies identifying the potential cost and schedule impacts of proposed technical changes.

Defining the project work is a four-step process of: (1) specifying the project objectives; (2) identifying specifically the products, services, or results (deliverables or end items) to be provided to the customer; (3) identifying work areas in the project that represent intermediate outputs or complement the deliverables; and (4) subdividing each of the Step 2 and 3 items into successive logical subcategories until the complexity and work effort in the elements become manageable units for planning and control purposes.[2]

At every level of the WBS, the sum of the child elements is 100 percent of the work represented by the parent element.

In the early phases of a project, developing a detailed WBS may not be feasible because the structure of the deliverables may yet be undefined. As the project progresses in the project feasibility phase or planning phase, the end products and the planning become more detailed. The subdivisions of the WBS are developed to successively lower levels at that time.

These final subcategories or work packages are the elements that will be used to perform the project work. The product of this "subcategorization" process is the completed work breakdown structure.

Because the WBS elements represent work or areas of work, not actions, they are normally stated as nouns or nouns and adjectives. (Activities represent action and normally include verbs in their descriptions.)

WBS Development Steps

The steps to develop a WBS can be illustrated by a specific example of a consulting study for a new project management control system for an IT organization:

Step 1. *Specify the project objectives*: Develop a project management and control methodology for the IT organization to facilitate the administration and oversight of each project to ensure achievement of the goals and objectives of each IT project.

Step 2. *Identify specifically the products, services, or results (deliverables or end items)*: Perform and document an assessment of current practices, prepare a set of recommendations, prepare an implementation plan, and train the project managers in the methodology.

Step 3. *Identify other work areas to make sure 100% of the work is identified*: A project management function is needed to do such things as prepare a project plan and schedule, hold a kickoff meeting, prepare progress reports, and administer in-process reviews.

Figure 3-2 shows the WBS so far.

Level 1 is the total project, and Level 2 is the subdivision into the final products (an assessment and set of recommendations and an implemented and operational system) as well as crosscutting or complementary work needed for the project, such as the project management function. The total scope of the project is represented by the sum of the work in the three Level 2 elements.

Step 4. Subdivide the elements until a level is achieved that is suitable for *planning and control*.

Figure 3-3 shows the next level subdivision of each Level 2 element.

At the next level below the work packages are the individual tasks or activities (see Figure 3-4). These are not normally considered a part of the

FIGURE 3-2   Top-Level Work Breakdown Structure

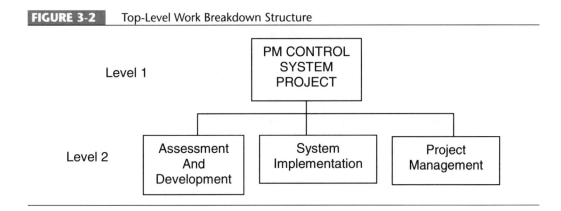

FIGURE 3-3   WBS to Level 3

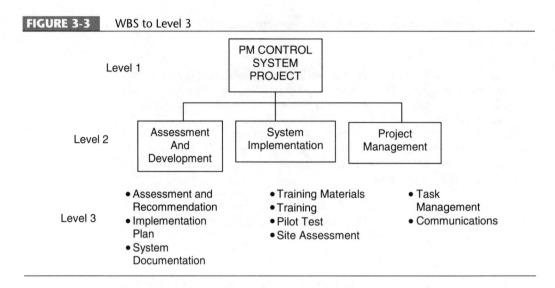

WBS. In fact, one of the primary uses of the WBS is to provide a framework to assist in defining the activities of the project.

Once the WBS is established it must be maintained and updated to reflect changes in the project. Work is added, deleted, changed, or clarified. The configuration and content of the WBS and the specific work packages vary from project to project depending on several considerations:

- Size and complexity of the project
- Structure of the organizations involved
- Phase of the project
- Product structure
- Project manager judgment of allocating work to subcontractors
- Degree of uncertainty and risk involved
- Time available for planning.

Although all projects are unique, the work in a particular organization is generally similar to work performed previously. The WBSs, therefore, lend themselves to being used as templates, at least at the upper levels, and therefore do not need to be reinvented each time a new, similar project is established.

Work Package Definition

The lowest level of the WBS is defined as the work package level. A work package provides a logical basis for defining activities or assigning responsibility to a specific person or organization. In Figure 3-4, for example, each of the lowest elements in each part of the WBS is a work package.

FIGURE 3-4   PM Control System Project Work Breakdown Structure

LEVEL 1	LEVEL 2	LEVEL 3	LEVEL 4	LEVEL 5
PM Control System Project	Assessment and Development	Assessment and Recommendation	Assessment	Interviews
				Assessment Report
			Recommendations	Recommendation Report
				Briefing
		Implementation Plan	Implementation Approach and Briefing	
			Implementation Plan	
		System Documentation		
	System Implementation	Training Materials	Visual Aids	
			Participant and Instructor Guides	
		Training	Pilot Test	
			Project Managers	
		Pilot Test	Pilot Test	
			Assessment	
		Site Assessment	Assessment Criteria	
			Assessment	
			Assessment Report	
	Project Management	Task Management	Kickoff Meeting	
			Project Plan	
		Communications	Reports	
			In-Process Reviews	
			Teleconferences	

"Recommendation Report" at Level 5 is a work package, as are "Pilot Test" at Level 4 with the parent of "Training" at Level 3. It is not necessary to decompose any work package to the next level. All provide a basis for defining activities and represent a single work area.

STEP 2: DEFINING THE ACTIVITIES OR TASKS—THE BASIC BUILDING BLOCKS

One of the most important steps is defining the project activities. This section describes the process and provides a list of activity characteristics.

Activity Definition

Activity definition involves identifying and documenting the specific activities that must be performed to produce the deliverables identified in the work breakdown structure and to perform the work represented in the work packages. A WBS is decomposed to the work package level. Below the work package level are the activities where the work is actually performed and network planning is accomplished. Activities represent action and are normally stated in verb/adjective/noun form. For example, for the work package "Visual Aids," the activities to be performed could be as follows:

1. Defining the visual aid requirements
2. Identifying the visual aids
3. Preparing graphics
4. Preparing draft visual aids
5. Testing visual aids
6. Preparing final visual aids
7. Completing visual aids (milestone).

Each activity has a specified and expected duration, resources, cost, performance, and output.

Figure 3-5 illustrates the relationship between the WBS, work packages, and activities for Project X, a new personal computer development project.

Cost estimation and planning is performed at the activity level. However, cost control is often impractical at the activity level because of the difficulty in collecting actual cost data. It usually can be exercised at the level above—the work package—or at a higher level.

The cost account (or control account) is the term used to describe the management control point at which actual cost can be accumulated and compared to budgeted costs for work performed. The value of the actual work performed is referred to as earned value, and the plan is referred to as planned value in earned value management systems.[3]

The use of the WBS to facilitate identifying and defining the activities that must be performed in the project is illustrated in Figures 3-6 and 3-7 for a hypothetical automated ordering system. In Figure 3-6, the WBS elements are in adjective/noun form. In Figure 3-7, the WBS elements are in bold. The activities are in italics in verb/adjective/noun form at the level below the WBS.

This example illustrates the relationship of the WBS to the activities. The individual activities are linked in the PM software into a precedence network; this is displayed in Gantt chart format on the screen and when printed out.

FIGURE 3-5   WBS, Work Package, and Activity Relationship

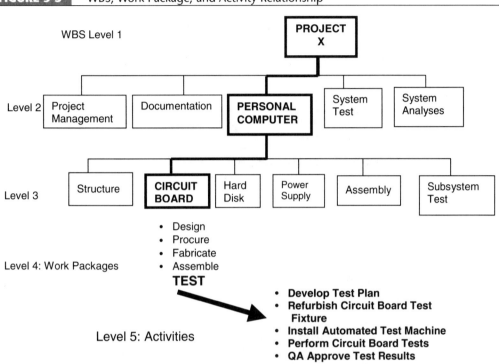

The manner in which the WBS is arrayed can make schedules easier to read and to use. Put the project management element at the top of the WBS and number it 1.0, as shown. If there is any natural process flow at Level 2 of the WBS, have it go from left to right in the graphic version of the WBS or from top to bottom in the outline version so that the schedules will be displayed more naturally.

Establishing a special work package under project management for the start and complete events of the project is a useful device to assist in scheduling. Included in that work package are the two zero-duration activities or milestones that identify the start and completion.

When the WBS data are entered into the project management software, identifying all the activities in the project and arraying them in a logical schedule format is easy and swift.

Activity Characteristics

Experience has shown that defining activities or tasks is not as easy as it looks. Too many times they are inadequately defined, resulting in poor schedules and communication problems. Activity definition is extremely

Examples of WBS Elements

WORK BREAKDOWN STRUCTURE

Automated Ordering System (AOS) Project

1.0 Project Management
- 1.1   **Project Start and Complete**
- 1.2   **Project Meetings**
- 1.3   **Project Reports**

2.0 AOS Requirements Specification
- 2.1   **Initial AOS Requirements Specification**
- 2.2   **Final AOS Requirements Specification**

3.0 AOS Design Specification
- 3.1   **Initial AOS Design Specification**
- 3.2   **Final AOS Design Specification**

4.0 AOS Software
- 4.1   **AOS Module 1**
- 4.2   **AOS Module 2**
- 4.3   **Module Integration**

---

important because activities are the basic building blocks for planning and controlling the project. Figure 3-8 is a comprehensive list of the characteristics of activities.

A very important consideration is that the reason to have a written plan or schedule is to make sure the need for the activity is communicated to the appropriate stakeholders, including those persons responsible for predecessor and successor activities as well as the person responsible for performing the activity. *The activity may not be performed if it is not in the plan.*

In Figure 3-7, the AOS Requirements Specification and the AOS Design Specification are well-defined documents, and the activities involved are all clear. The outputs are tangible—something is done to the document. The activities of coding the software are similarly clearly defined. The output would be completed software code, probably hard copy as well as digital form, depending on the normal practices of the organization. Unit test is usually defined with the completion of a document provided by the quality control organization or someone providing a similar independent function.

STEP 3: DEVELOPING THE NETWORK DIAGRAM

In the third step, the identified activities must be sequenced and the relationships identified to support later development of a realistic and achiev-

FIGURE 3-7   Example of WBS Elements and Activities

WORK BREAKDOWN STRUCTURE AND ACTIVITIES

Automated Ordering System (AOS) Project

1.0   Project Management
    1.1   Project Start and Complete
        1.1.1   Go Ahead
        1.1.2   Complete Project
    1.2   Project Meetings
        1.2.1   Prepare for Kickoff Meeting
        1.2.2   Start Kickoff Meeting
    1.3   Project Reports
        1.3.1   Prepare Interim Progress Report
        1.3.2   Deliver Interim Progress Report
2.0   AOS Requirements Specification
    2.1   Initial AOS Requirements Specification
        2.1.1   Create Initial AOS Requirements Specification
        2.1.2   Review Initial AOS Requirements Specification
        2.1.3   Update Initial AOS Requirements Specification
    2.2   Final AOS Requirements Specification
        2.2.1   Review Final AOS Requirements Specification
        2.2.2   Approve Final AOS Requirements Specification
3.0   AOS Design Specification
    3.1   Initial AOS Design Specification
        3.1.1   Create Initial AOS Design Specification
        3.1.2   Review Initial AOS Design Specification
        3.1.3   Update Initial AOS Design Specification
    3.2   Final AOS Design Specification
        3.2.1   Review Final AOS Design Specification
        3.2.2   Approve Final AOS Design Specification
4.0   AOS Software
    4.1   AOS Module 1
        4.1.1   Code AOS Module 1
        4.1.2   Unit Test AOS Module 1
    4.2   AOS Module 2
        4.2.1   Code AOS Module 2
        4.2.2   Unit Test AOS Module 2
    4.3   Module Integration
        4.3.1   System Test Integrated Modules
        4.3.2   Complete AOS Software

---

able schedule. This process generally is performed using project management software, but manual techniques also may be used. Several items affect activity sequencing and interdependence:

1. Product description—product characteristics, such as the physical layout of a plant to be constructed or a subsystem interface on a software product, may affect activity sequencing.

FIGURE 3-8 Activity Characteristics

ACTIVITY CHARACTERISTICS

Work is performed and described in terms of a verb, adjective, and noun—there is action performed.

A single person or organization is responsible for the work—more than one resource may be assigned to an activity, but one person is in charge of delivering the output. If this is not the case, the item needs further decomposition or joint responsibilities clarified.

It has a defined start point—there is a specific action that can be identified that marks the start of an activity or a predecessor activity that must be completed.

There is a tangible output or product at completion (usually)—projects occasionally have level-of-effort activities or support activities without clearly defined outputs; however, the primary activities have defined and measurable outputs. The point at which an activity is completed is determined by the availability of an output product that is used as input by a successor activity.

It fits logically under an existing WBS element—if it does not, then either the activity is not part of the project, the WBS needs modification, or the activity is ambiguous and needs redefinition.

It is of a size and duration that is sufficient for control—activities that are too long do not provide sufficient time for corrective action if problems arise, and too many activities that are too short can make the cost of the control more expensive than a problem that may arise; however, using a rolling wave concept where the near-term activities are relatively short and those many months in the future are larger, summary activities makes sense.

Actual schedule status data can be collected for the activity—for schedule control, the start and end points must be sufficiently defined that the start and finish of the activity can be reported.

Actual cost (person-hour) data can be collected for the activity or work package that contains the activity—for cost or resource control, actual cost data or the actual expenditure of resources can be collected; obviously, if tracking actual expenditures is not required, this principle can be ignored.

The labor and costs necessary to perform the activity can be estimated—the resource requirements must be able to be determined in the planning phase.

The activity represents a significant effort in support of project objectives—trivial or incidental activities need not be included.

Zero-duration activities are milestones or events and represent the start or completion of another activity or set of activities—They should be included at the start and finish of the project and included to identify completion of key activities or groups of activities.

2. Mandatory dependencies—those dependencies that are inherent in the nature of the work underway. They often involve physical limitations such as the availability of a specific test facility in which to perform a test.

3. Discretionary dependencies—those that are defined by the project management team, such as deciding not to start a series of activities until after moving into new office space.

4. External dependencies—those that involve an external interface with other projects. For example, the testing activity in a software project may be dependent on delivery of hardware from another project, research data from one project are to be used by several other projects, or the customer for a project is to provide certain information or equipment necessary for the work on the project.

Networking Procedures

Chapter 2 discusses the various types of networks: PERT/CPM and PDM. This chapter describes the steps involved in developing a network following the precedence or PDM approach. Figure 3-9 shows a sample of a precedence network for a simple project.

If drawing the network manually, start with the list of activities derived from the WBS and follow the rules outlined below. These also apply if project management software is used.

| FIGURE 3-9 | Sample Precedence Network |

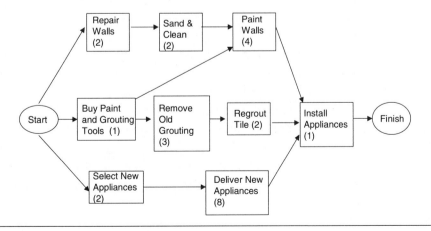

Kitchen Remodeling Project
PDM Network

1. Activities are shown as rectangles; the left end represents the start of the activity, and the right end represents its completion.
2. The arrows between the activities are constraints and identify only the activity relationships; they do not represent work being accomplished.
3. An arrow from one activity to another means that the successor activity *cannot* start until the predecessor activity is complete.
4. If the activity has more than one predecessor, it cannot start until all the predecessor activities are completed.

The four types of relationships between activities in a PDM network are:

1. Finish-to-Start—the most common when the succeeding activity cannot start until the preceding activity has been completed.
2. Finish-to-Finish—occurs when the succeeding activity cannot finish until the preceding activity has been completed. The two activities may finish together.
3. Start-to-Start—occurs when the succeeding activity cannot start until the preceding activity has started. Two activities may start simultaneously.
4. Start-to-Finish—occurs when the succeeding activity's finish is based on the start of a preceding activity. This relationship occurs rarely.

These are illustrated in Figure 3-10. It is assumed that the left edge of the activity box represents the start and the right edge represents the finish. It is not correct to show the linkages from the horizontal centers of the boxes because then the nature of the relationship is unclear.

Dependency arrows do not normally indicate the use of time and are of zero duration. However, if a delay (lag) is to be scheduled or expected between two activities, the appropriate duration should be added to the constraint. The lag may be negative in some situations.

Start-to-start and finish-to-finish constraints are used when related activities proceed in parallel. Also known as partial dependencies, these are illustrated in Figure 3-11.

In this example, the activity detail design must start before the activity assembly design. The assembly design does not have to wait until all the detail design work is completed but could start immediately after detail design starts. Similarly, assembly design cannot finish until detail design finishes. Both the start-to-start and finish-to-finish constraints are candidates for lag times being added.

FIGURE 3-10 Task Relationships

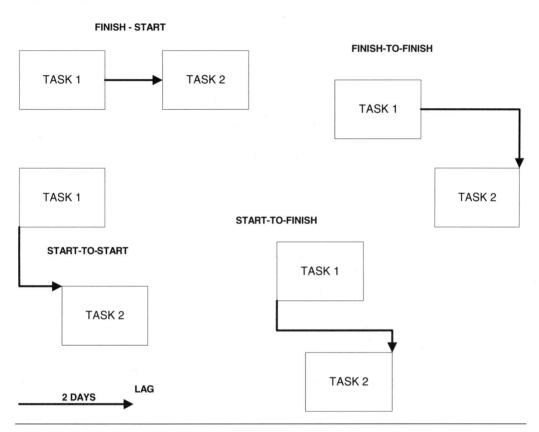

Activity networks are not a flowchart with process steps; they have no feedback loops, which would imply time flowing backward. Activities that must be repeated should be duplicated if this is planned or the activity added when the necessity to repeat becomes apparent. This might occur if a qualification or acceptance test failure occurs and the test has to be repeated.

Use of PM Software for Network Development

It is much easier to use PM software for network planning than to do it manually. The process is very simple; the key is to use the WBS as the framework.

As a first step, enter the WBS into the PM software using the Gantt display. The next step is to define the activities under each *lowest* WBS element. You will discover that with a little practice you can define the activities

FIGURE 3-11 Partial Dependencies

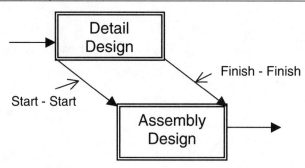

faster than you can type, and in a very short time you will have defined all the activities on the project. This assumes, of course, that you have a complete WBS for the project and an understanding of the work to be performed. At the same time you are defining the activities, it is possible to perform Step 3—Developing the Network Diagram, Step 4—Estimating Activity Duration, and Step 5—Estimating Resource Requirements concurrently (see Figure 3-1).

All project management software packages have the capability of linking the activities using any of the four different activity relationship possibilities shown in Figure 3-10. Such software usually has two or more methods of linking the activities, such as by identifying the predecessor activity numbers, by pointing and clicking with the mouse, or by other commands.

An important rule is to make sure that all the predecessors are identified for each activity. It is recommended that a "start" milestone or equivalent be shown under the project management WBS and that all activities that can begin when this occurs are linked to it. One of the practical reasons is that if the start date is changed, only one date needs to be changed in the computer and the network will be shifted in time as required.

Using a default duration of either zero or one day is recommended for all activities because it is easy to identify activities whose durations have not yet been estimated. Also, it makes it easy to identify activities whose predecessors have not yet been identified and linked because they will all be shown at "time now" or "start," depending on how you have instructed the software. Some persons have discovered that when using the software, it is easier to estimate activity durations before linking, which involves combining Steps 3 and 4 of Figure 3-1.

In Figure 3-12, the data of Figure 3-7 have been entered into MS Project 98® to illustrate the use of the WBS as an outline for developing the activi-

FIGURE 3-12 WBS Elements and Activities in MS Project 98®

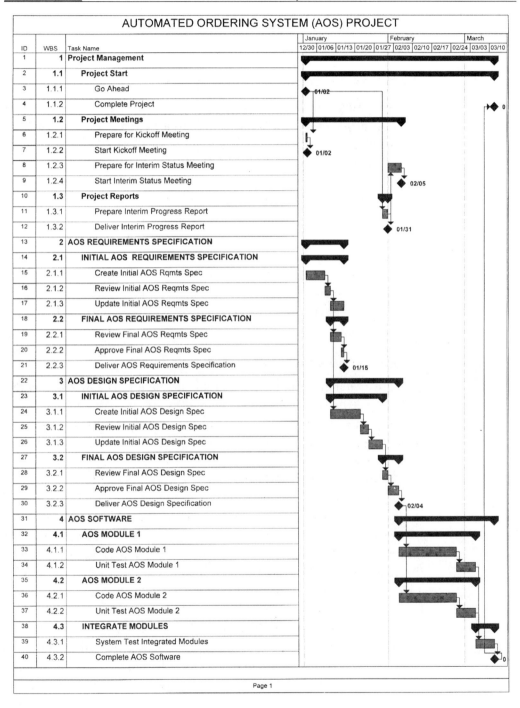

ties and structuring the schedule. The WBS elements are in bold, and the related activities are indented under the lowest WBS elements. Linkages are shown on the Gantt display but can be hidden to print a cleaner-looking document.

STEP 4: ESTIMATING ACTIVITY DURATIONS

Estimating activity duration involves assessing the number of work periods (time) needed to complete each identified activity. It is recommended that the person or group on the project team who is most familiar with the nature of a specific activity make or at least approve the duration estimate.

To estimate duration, historical data, expert judgment, experience, and analogous estimating processes may be used. Information may be available from project files or commercial databases, but most often from the knowledge of project team members. Constraints and assumptions should be considered. Sometimes activity durations are set in advance or fixed, and the estimating involves determining the resources necessary to complete the activity within the set time.

There are several different philosophies and methods of determining activity duration.

Elapsed Time versus Work Time

Activity duration can be stated in minutes, hours, days, weeks, months, or any other time unit. In using computer software to assist in planning and scheduling, it is often possible to intermix the units; the computer software then adjusts to a default time period that has been established. Project duration would be the length of time to complete the entire project or to deliver the primary end item.

When planning the project in the feasibility and planning phases of the lifecycle, it is customary to express activity durations in terms of *elapsed time* or *calendar time* in a Gantt format. These activity durations would include weekends, holidays, vacations, plant shutdown periods, and the like. Customers will usually express project durations in elapsed time; these units are used in contracts and requests for proposals when specific dates are not feasible. For example, it is common to see that the delivery of an end item is stated as so many days or weeks after "CA" (contract award), "NTP" (notice to proceed), or simply "days after award." Unless stated otherwise, these terms represent normally elapsed time or calendar time.

Certain types of activities are also always expressed in elapsed time due to their nature. Common examples are concrete drying or paint drying.

The duration also is expressed in elapsed time when renting facilities or equipment.

When estimating the duration of individual activities, however, it is normal to use working time. This is essential when using bottom-up cost estimating, which is based on adding up the costs of individual activities to determine total project cost, because estimating is done in time units and the cost is determined by applying a labor rate to the units.

When preparing the schedule in Gantt format or assigning specific calendar dates, non-working periods must be considered. The specific dates depend on the consideration of non-work days and whether or not there is a holiday in the planned time period. Project management software contains a calendar that defines which days are non-work days and holidays, and will automatically account for these.

Effort-Driven versus Fixed-Duration Activities

There are two different approaches to determining the duration of activities: (1) effort-driven, which is based on the amount of work involved; and (2) fixed-duration, when the time span is predetermined. A combination of these is often used on the same project.

Effort-Driven Activity Duration

Effort-based activity durations require two data elements: (1) the estimated effort in terms such as person-hours or person-days, and (2) the number of persons assigned to the activity. If the estimate is 80 person-hours for an activity and two persons are assigned, the activity duration is 40 hours, 5 days, or one workweek. If only one person is assigned, the activity will take 80 hours, 10 days, or two weeks.

The availability of resources influences the duration of activities and therefore the schedule. A key person on vacation or a trip in support of another project affects the schedule. Project management software sometimes contains calendars for individual resources that allow consideration of key personnel availability in establishing activity duration or schedules.

Fixed-Duration Activities

Fixed-duration activities approach the time dimension with a different philosophy than the effort-driven model. In this model, the activity duration is set first and then the resources are assigned to complete the activity in the predetermined time. There are three variations of the fixed-duration activity model:

Time-Critical Activities—For activities whose fixed durations are critical to meeting project delivery requirements, the resources are assigned to perform the required activity in the established time period. Multiple quantities of a given resource may be required to complete it in the assigned time. For example, three engineers may be required to complete an engineering activity within a specified time, or five painters may be needed for a construction activity.

A difficulty is that resources are not always equally productive, and doubling the number of persons may not reduce the duration by half—the same problem as the effort-driven activities. Adding resources to shorten the duration only works when the work can be subdivided into smaller packages that can be worked in parallel. Painting a room can be subdivided into the four walls and ceiling, and five (or more) persons can be working at once. Adding more resources cannot shorten activities when the details must be accomplished in series. Substituting more productive resources or increasing the workday shortens these.

On the surface this situation seems analogous to the effort-driven model, but conceptually it is different. Usually, the customer or sponsor has established total project duration, or delivery of a product is required on a certain date. The schedule is established by fitting the activities into the available time. Resources are assigned to match the activity durations, and a trial-and-error process (including a lot of experience) is used to balance required activity durations and resources.

Non–Time-Critical Activities—In the case of non–time-critical activities, the activity durations are established as above (to fit a specified project duration). Many of the activity durations are longer than required considering the nature of the work or the number of person-hours actually required or estimated.

The non-critical items could include an activity such as writing a test plan. The actual writing may be estimated to take only 40 hours, but three weeks are shown on the schedule. The person is assigned one-third time to the activity, or 40 hours. When the person works on the report is not considered important as long as the activity is finished by the due date and does not require more than 40 hours. This gives the worker the flexibility to support more than one project and to balance his or her own workload.

Master Schedule Activities—A master schedule is the top-level schedule for a project that contains the project deliverables and the time spans allocated for the major project activities. It also includes major milestones established by the customer or the project manager and the major interfaces between organizations. In a master schedule, many of the activities are the equivalent of time budgets, and the organization responsible is expected to complete all the work within the specified time span.

For example, an engineering organization is assigned (and agrees to) a certain period for a work package, such as design of a major assembly. This time period is reflected in the master schedule Gantt chart as a single bar. The engineering organization, performing its internal planning and considering resource availability and other project commitments, develops detailed schedules of the work to be performed in the design of the components that comprise the assembly and the design of the assembly.

Each functional organization would develop its schedule similarly based on the negotiated activity durations in the master schedule.

Activity Duration Estimation—PERT

Activities represent the work necessary to proceed from one event to another in the PERT algorithm and thus require the expenditure of time and resources. Each activity is assigned three time values:

1. *Optimistic*: A minimum time that is attainable only when unusually good performance is achieved and having no more than one chance in a hundred of being lessened.
2. *Most Likely*: A probable time that would reasonably be expected by the person best qualified to judge and would occur most often if the activity could be repeated numerous times under the same conditions.
3. *Pessimistic*: A maximum time that can occur only if unusually bad performance is experienced and having no more than one chance in a hundred of being exceeded. The pessimistic time should reflect the possibility of initial failure and a fresh start. It is not influenced by such factors as the possibility of strikes, floods, fires, etc., unless such hazards are inherent to the activity.

Some of the other basic criteria for the estimating process are:

• All three estimates are based on the same level of effort. For example, all three estimates must be based on using the same number of persons working the same number of shifts and days per week. The three estimates provide a measure of the range caused by the uncertainties in a project activity. Basing each estimate on a different level of effort would really be estimating three different plans.

• The time estimates for each activity should be made or approved by the individual responsible for the work performed in the activity.

- The estimates must be determined independently of other network activities. Whether predecessor activities are more or less uncertain is not relevant.

The expected duration of an activity is based on the following formula:

$$t_e = (a + 4m + b)/6$$

where
a is the optimistic estimate
m is the most likely time, and
b is the pessimistic estimate.

Figure 3-13 presents a classic PERT network of the sample kitchen remodeling project of Figure 3-9, showing the three time estimates on the activities. Only "real" activities, that is, those that are bounded by start and complete events with the same description, get estimated. Dummy activities do not get estimated unless specific lag times are being scheduled, as discussed previously.

Activity Duration in Critical Chain Project Management

One of the key differences between traditional project management as presented in the *PMBOK® Guide* and *Critical Chain Project Management* is the philosophy of determining activity duration and using it in the calculation of total project completion time. Projects have what Goldratt describes as a common cause variation in the performance time of activities. This variation represents uncertainty in the activity performance time, which is inherent in the system of estimation. Although the time to perform individual activities is independent, project activity networks establish the activity dependence. Successor activities cannot start until predecessor activities are completed.

Figure 3-14 illustrates the typical project activity performance time distribution. The curve shows the probability of completing the activity in a time less than or equal to the time on the abscissa (the *x* axis). These figures represent the areas under the curve. The curve shows simply that there is a minimum time below which the probability of completing the activity is zero, and, as longer time is allowed, the probability of completing the activity by that time is increased. The peak of the chart is the "most likely time" referred to in the PERT section above.

This chart also matches our common sense: Activities have an absolute minimum time as indicated by the left end of the curve and a long tail to

FIGURE 3-13 Classic PERT Network Kitchen Remodeling Project

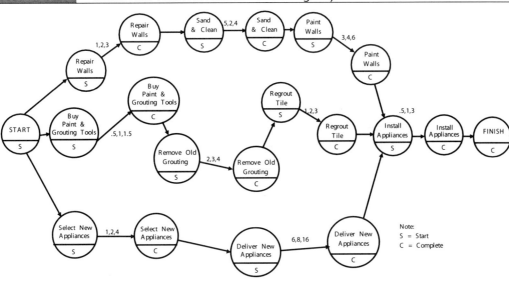

the right, meaning that they can take much longer than the average time. Goldratt and other CCPM authors contend that most activity duration estimating is approximately 90 percent accurate.

The curve illustrates that low-risk estimates (90 percent) can be much longer than the 50 percent probability estimate—as much as two to three times longer. One of the reasons is that everyone is more comfortable when

FIGURE 3-14 Common Cause Variation Activity Duration

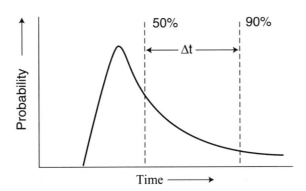

schedules are met; therefore, there is always a bias toward low-risk estimates. Further, the penalties of being late are sometimes severe, so it is human nature to build in a contingency plan.

Statistically, activities should finish early some percentage of time based on the probabilities. If estimates are 50 percent probable, people should finish early 50 percent of the time; if they are 90 percent probable, people should finish early 90 percent of the time. However, they do not, for several good reasons:

- People in high demand are often given other assignments. Because these people are usually the ones working on critical path activities, this can have a potentially serious impact.
- People take on other assignments because they have "free time," especially at the beginning of a master schedule–type activity.
- A phenomenon that Goldratt calls the "student syndrome" occurs. No matter how much time is allotted, students (workers) tend to start the work, then wait until it is almost due before they resume the work necessary to finish, leaving no time to recover if problems arise.
- Parkinson's Law: work expands to fill the additional time.

A related problem is failure to pass on positive variation when an activity is finished early. There are many reasons for persons not delivering work early. Many are related to the organization's culture: There may be no reward for finishing early, and doing so may in fact be detrimental to the worker. For example:

- With time-and-material contracts, finishing early may result in a loss in revenue.
- If you finish early, you may also have an underrun, and your budget may be cut.
- You may not have a project to which to charge your time, and charging to "overhead" may cause problems.
- Additional work may be assigned unfairly.

Alternatives include inefficiency, filling time with unproductive activities, or gold-plating the product, all of which result in using up contingency time unproductively.

This discussion of CCPM is abbreviated, focusing only on activity duration. Additional discussion is included in Chapter 4.

STEP 5: ESTIMATING THE RESOURCE REQUIREMENTS

Resources are required to perform the work on projects. They require estimation and planning to identify their quantity and timing.

Resource Tables

When using computer software to assist in project scheduling, and activity durations must be estimated, the resources to be assigned to the activity should be estimated at the same time. Activity durations and assigned resources are closely related.

A useful tool in assigning resources to activities is a resource table such as the one illustrated in Figure 3-15. Even if you are performing the analyses and planning manually, such a table is useful to consolidate resource data.

Most project management software programs contain a resource table that must be set up if resources or costs are to be managed. It may contain more data elements than the basic table outlined in Figure 3-15. It is either prepared in advance or developed as you identify the resources assigned to each activity. In organizations performing resource planning across projects, a common resource table for labor is used by all the project managers and administrators. In these situations, specific names of personnel working on the projects are often used in the table.

To develop a total cost estimate or a total resource plan, the resources to be used by *each* activity must be identified. There are no shortcuts.

For personnel planning and scheduling, the time required of persons who are not charging their costs to the project but who are needed for the project work also must be identified. They would be shown with a $0.00 cost rate in the table. The purpose of the "Quantity Available" column is to allow

FIGURE 3-15   Sample Resource Table

RESOURCE TABLE			
NAME	**TYPE**	**QUANTITY AVAILABLE**	**COST RATE**
Project Manager	Labor	1	$70.00 per hour
Architect	Labor	1	$60.00 per hour
Cabinets	Fixed Cost	1 Set	$4,000
Masons	Labor	2	$30.00 per hour
Automobile Travel	Unit Cost		$0.32 per mile
Plywood	Unit Cost		$15.00 per sheet
Laborers	Labor	5	$10.00 per hour
Paint	Unit Cost		$45.00 per gallon
Rental Car	Time Cost		$50.00 per day
Etc.			

the computer software or the manager to allocate additional personnel when effort-driven activities are critical or if there are resource conflicts.

Once the required resources for all the activities have been estimated, the total cost can be calculated and the assignment of personnel planned. It is not unusual for the first iteration to have resource and overloading conflicts or for the total cost and overall duration to exceed targets. The project must be re-planned and re-estimated as necessary to fit within the given constraints. If this is not possible, then the scope or project objectives may need to be changed.

Resource Histograms

The resource histogram is a useful tool for presenting and analyzing resource loading data on a project. Histograms can identify where individual resources are overloaded (or underutilized) so that appropriate adjustments to the plan can be accomplished and the person-power "smoothed." In the example shown in Figure 3-16, Marcia has no assignments on the project on June 1 and is assigned half time on June 2 and 3 and full time on June 4–8. She is overloaded on June 9–12, then back to half time on June 15. Non-work days are shown in gray. With these data and the data identifying the activities Marcia is assigned to for June 9–12, appropriate changes in plans or assignments can be made.

On larger projects, or when integrated multiple projects are managed, skill categories such as "test engineers" or "CICS programmers" are used and the histograms are analyzed to determine hiring (or downsizing) needs.

STEP 6: DEVELOPING THE SCHEDULE

Schedule development means determining planned start and finish dates for all project activities. If the start and finish dates are not realistic, the project is high risk or uneconomic.

FIGURE 3-16   Resource Histogram—Marcia

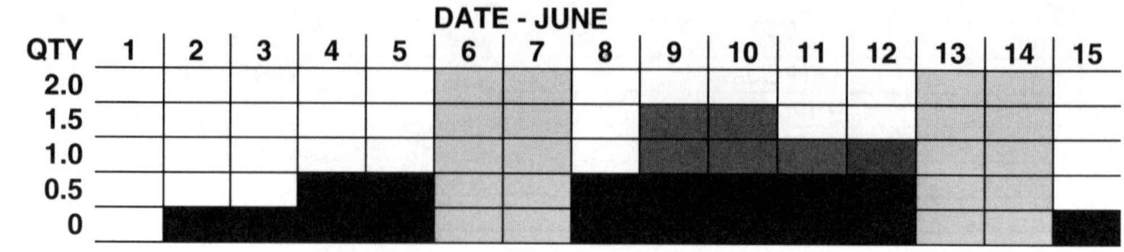

Schedule development proceeds using the project network diagram, duration estimates, resource availability, project and resource calendars to identify non-work days, and various other constraints. These constraints can include imposed dates, key events, major milestones, and interfacing projects. The project sponsor, customer, or other stakeholders may require completion of certain deliverables by a specified date, or they may be furnishing equipment or may require approval of certain items before the project can proceed. Particular attention also must be paid to the reliability of any resource or activity duration assumptions, as invalid assumptions later become problems.

Project management software should be used to assist with developing schedules. These products automate the calculations of mathematical analysis and allow consideration of many schedule alternatives. They also help prepare graphical descriptions of the project schedules in varying levels of detail, including project network diagrams and Gantt charts.

PDM and CPM/PERT Calculations

The purpose of the calculations is to determine the overall project duration, the critical paths, and the amount of float or slack in the non-critical paths. The critical path by definition is the longest path through the network, and float or slack is the amount of time available on other paths before they become critical. These data are important in developing an effective and efficient schedule.

Following are the instructions for calculating the network when performing the process manually. Figure 3-17 will be used as an example. The PDM network has been developed and the durations of each activity estimated.

The calculations are performed in three steps: a forward pass, a backward pass, and float or slack. The purposes are to determine the earliest time each activity can start and complete, thereby determining the total project duration, and to determine the schedule critical and non-critical activities and paths.

Forward Pass

In the forward pass, the earliest start and finish times for each activity and event are worked out as follows:
1. Calculate earliest start (ES) and earliest finish (EF) times for each activity based on estimated activity durations, starting at the first (left-most) event.
   a) The first activity will have an earliest start time of zero. The earliest finish time of the first task will be equal to the activity duration.

FIGURE 3-17 PDM Network Diagram

Kitchen Remodeling Project

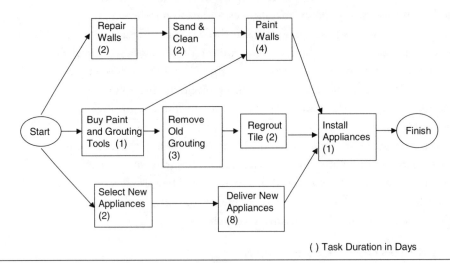

( ) Task Duration in Days

---

    b) Transfer the earliest finish time to the next activity. This will become its earliest start time.

    c) Add the activity duration for the activity to the earliest start time to get the earliest finish time.

2. Where there is a choice, i.e., multiple constraints, transfer the longer time. The reason is that the activity cannot start until all predecessor activities are complete; therefore, the latest completion time drives the schedule.

3. Write the earliest start time and the earliest finish time for each activity above the upper left-hand and upper right-hand corners of the activity box.

Figure 3-18 illustrates these calculations.

Backward Pass

In the backward pass, the latest start and finish times are calculated for each activity and event to determine how late each activity could be performed without adversely affecting the project completion time calculated in the forward pass:

1. For the last activity or event in the networks, set the latest finish time (LF) equal to the earliest finish time (EF) for that activity or event as calculated in the forward pass.

2. Starting at the last (right-most) activity, and working from right to left, calculate the latest finish time and the latest start time for each

---

FIGURE 3-18 Forward Pass Calculations

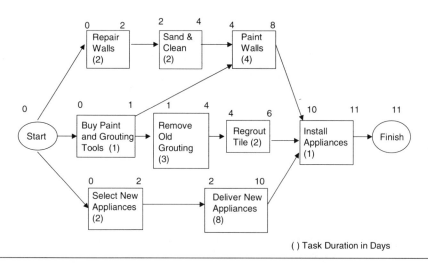

Kitchen Remodeling Project
PDM Network—ES & EF Calculations

( ) Task Duration in Days

activity based on estimated activity durations. Subtract the activity duration from the latest finish time to get the latest start time for each activity. The latest start transfers as the latest finish for the next activity.

3. Where there is a choice, i.e., multiple constraints, transfer the shorter time because this would represent the latest time the activity can start and complete.

4. Write the latest finish times and earliest start times for each activity below the activity boxes at the corners.

Figure 3-19 illustrates the backward pass calculations.

Float or Slack

The third set of calculations determines the amount of float or slack associated with each activity:

1. The arithmetic difference between the earliest start and the latest start or the earliest finish and the latest finish of each activity is called "float" or "slack." Calculate this difference for each activity, write it below the activity, and circle it.

2. The "critical path" is the longest path through the network and also has zero float or slack. Mark the critical path with heavy arrows.

3. More than one "critical path" may exist. However, there is always at least one critical path.

FIGURE 3-19
Backward Pass Calculations

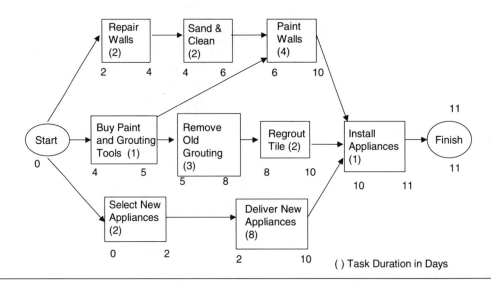

Kitchen Remodeling Project
PDM Network—LS & LF Calculations

( ) Task Duration in Days

Figure 3-20 illustrates all the calculations and the calculation of slack or float. The critical path is marked.

In Figure 3-20, a choice had to be made for the ES of "Install Appliances"; this followed the rule that where there is a choice, the longer time is selected. Also, there was a choice for the LF of "Buy Paint and Grouting Tools" in the backward pass. The rule stating that when there is a choice, the shorter time is transferred, was followed. The total project duration is in working days. Weekends and holidays would be considered when relating the data to specific calendar dates.

Six new terms have been introduced:

Early Start (ES)—the earliest time an activity can start considering the logic constraints and activity durations.

Early Finish (EF)—the earliest time an activity can finish considering the logic constraints and activity durations.

Late Start (LS)—the latest time an activity can start and not affect the calculated total duration of the project.

Late Finish (LF)—the latest time an activity can finish and not affect the calculated total duration of the project.

Critical Path—the longest path through the network.

Float or Slack—the amount of time an activity can move without affecting the total project duration.

FIGURE 3-20   Critical Path and Slack

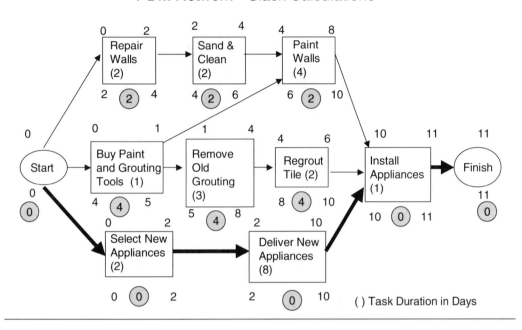

Kitchen Remodeling Project
PDM Network—Slack Calculations

Figure 3-21 presents the data in Gantt format using MS Project 98© software. The constraints between activities are shown to illustrate the format.

Calculating Critical Path and Float

Figure 3-22 presents the network calculations of the kitchen remodeling project. In this case, the ES, EF, LS, and LF schedule dates for the project are illustrated. The project management software converts the data to dates based on a given project start date and a master calendar identifying non-work days.

Project management software normally schedules each activity to be performed as soon as possible (ASAP), regardless of the amount of slack. It is also possible to schedule activities to be performed as late as possible (ALAP), in which case all the paths would be equally critical. Other criteria can be used on an activity-by-activity basis and include: "start no later than ____," "start no earlier than ____," and "start on ____," where specific dates are assigned to the activity.

FIGURE 3-21   Gantt Chart Schedule

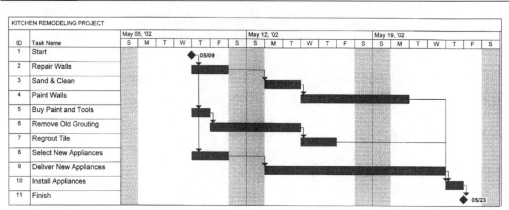

The critical path activities are readily identified in Figure 3-22, as they are the activities where the total slack is "0," or where the difference between the ES and LS or EF and LF is zero, as discussed in Chapter 3.

Figure 3-22 includes two columns labeled "total slack" and "free slack." These are also referred to as "total float" and "free float" based on the terminology used originally in CPM.

"Total slack or total float" refers to the amount of slack on the path where the particular activity is located and is the type of slack calculated in Figure 3-20. The "0" slack activities define the critical path. To reduce the overall project schedule duration, one or more of these activities must be shortened. The next most critical path has two days' slack; therefore, if the critical path is reduced by two days, this next path also becomes critical.

"Free slack or free float" represents the amount an activity can be delayed without affecting the start of any succeeding activity. It can be seen graphically on Figure 3-22 that Activity 7, "Regrout Tile," has four days' free slack and therefore can move four days without affecting another activity start.

Setting Standard Milestones

Some organizations have developed a standard format or template for reporting the status of major projects. They establish a standard set of major milestones that are to be included on all schedules of a certain type or when above a specified dollar threshold. Other milestones are added to the report as necessary for the specific project. These milestones are also used as the basis for progress payments when the work is contracted out. Schedule data to be

FIGURE 3-22   Network Calculations

ID	Task Name	Early Start	Early Finish	Late Start	Late Finish	Total Slack	Free Slack
	KITCHEN REMODELING PROJECT						
1	Start	05/09/02	05/09/02	05/09/02	05/09/02	0 days	0 days
2	Repair Walls	05/09/02	05/10/02	05/13/02	05/14/02	2 days	0 days
3	Sand & Clean	05/13/02	05/14/02	05/15/02	05/16/02	2 days	0 days
4	Paint Walls	05/15/02	05/20/02	05/17/02	05/22/02	2 days	2 days
5	Buy Paint and Tools	05/09/02	05/09/02	05/20/02	05/20/02	7 days	7 days
6	Remove Old Grouting	05/10/02	05/14/02	05/16/02	05/20/02	4 days	0 days
7	Regrout Tile	05/15/02	05/16/02	05/21/02	05/22/02	4 days	4 days
8	Select New Appliances	05/09/02	05/10/02	05/09/02	05/10/02	0 days	0 days
9	Deliver New Appliances	05/13/02	05/22/02	05/13/02	05/22/02	0 days	0 days
10	Install Appliances	05/23/02	05/23/02	05/23/02	05/23/02	0 days	0 days
11	Finish	05/23/02	05/23/02	05/23/02	05/23/02	0 days	0 days

reported for each milestone include the original schedule date, the current schedule date, and the forecast schedule date. The standard milestones used by a major transit organization that does a lot of construction are identified in Figure 3-23.

These standard milestones have very specific definitions that are used companywide. The standard milestones are required in all project schedules and in the monthly reports to higher management.

Establishing Check Points and Performance Measures

An important element of a project management methodology is establishing checkpoints and performance measurement metrics. Every project has certain critical check points (CCPs) when major decisions are made or major milestones reached. These often occur at merge points in networks. These are the points where management attention must be focused as the project is implemented. These CCPs should be identified, successful performance defined, variance limits and metrics established, and the mechanisms to measure performance relative to the CCPs established. Schedule risk analyses are conducted at these CCPs.

Other performance measures also should be developed that depend on the nature of the project, such as the use of "earned value" techniques for

FIGURE 3-23 Standard Milestones

PROGRESS MILESTONES	
PHASE	**MILESTONE**
PRE-DESIGN	Field Trip Scheduled Draft Scope Complete Approved Scope RFP Issued Consultant or A&E Contractor Selected Negotiations Complete Willingness to Assume Responsibility Approved Staff Summary Sheet Approved
DESIGN	Design Start Schematic Stage Complete Preliminary Stage Complete Advanced Stage Complete Final Stage Complete Design Complete Funding Available Advertise Bid Openings Staff Summary Sheet Approved
CONSTRUCTION	Award Complete Beneficial Use Date Subcontracts Complete Final Punch List Construction Complete Final Documentation Accept Claims Received Extension of Time Granted Engineering Audit Final Completion Certificate of Completion
CLOSE-OUT	Close-out Complete

larger projects. The use of the earned value management system can provide a continuous measure of performance of the total project or of selected areas. Other performance measures must be consistent with the product and the culture of the organization.

Rolling Wave

The process of planning and scheduling involves predicting the future. It is usually unwarranted to schedule many months into the future at a very detailed level.

Figure 3-24 shows an example of a three-month detailed schedule. Because of the number of activities associated with some projects, it is common practice to prepare an overall summary schedule or master schedule for a project and then to prepare detailed schedules only for the next three or six months. Details are shown for each week in the project over this period. Details are added to summary WBS elements and activities at regular intervals as the project progresses. This approach is known as the "rolling wave" technique. Detailed activities, scheduled many months or even years in advance, will not remain unchanged, and it is counterproductive to prepare detailed schedules only to have to change them frequently.

STEP 7: ESTABLISHING THE BASELINE SCHEDULE AND BUDGET

The final step in the planning and scheduling process is establishing a coordinated and approved schedule referred to as the "baseline." Establishing

FIGURE 3-24   Rolling Wave Schedule

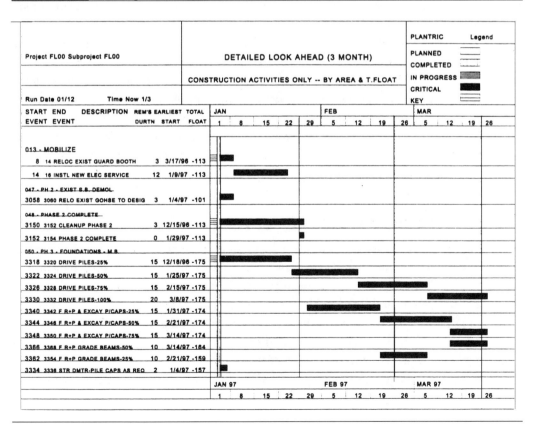

a baseline officially marks the end of the planning phase and the beginning of implementation. The purpose of the baseline is to establish an agreed-upon project schedule that can be used as the basis for work authorization, budgeting, and control. It must be coordinated with all stakeholders, especially the customer/sponsor and organizations providing resources to support the schedule. Although there may need to be changes to it as the project progresses, the original baseline schedule should be retained for analysis and future planning.

The baseline schedule is often a major component of a project plan, which includes supporting narrative information. The project plan is described below.

Once the logic network and associated resources are adjusted to meet the project schedule and cost objectives, the results can be "baselined." Using project management software, this usually is performed by entering a command to establish a baseline. The schedule and resource configuration are "frozen" but are available for comparison to actual performance. These data then are issued as the official master schedule and budget to all organizations involved in the project.

Schedules are normally issued in Gantt chart format such as described in Chapter 2.

The project manager must tightly control changes to the baseline. Other types of changes, such as actual completion dates for activities and actual resource expenditures, do not change the baseline data. Comparisons to the baseline are readily available for variance analysis, corrective action assignments, and graphic presentations. Changes to the baseline usually are accompanied by a change in scope and concurred with by the project sponsor or customer.

PREPARING THE PROJECT PLAN

Chapter 1 contains a discussion of the importance of planning and the reasons to plan. These reasons apply to project plans. A project plan is a formal approved document that is prepared during the planning phase of a project and frequently identifies the end of the planning phase.

There are seven general reasons to prepare a project plan:
1. To guide project execution
2. To eliminate or reduce uncertainty
3. To document project planning assumptions, constraints, and decisions

4. To document functional department support commitments
5. To gain and communicate a better understanding of the project objectives
6. To provide a basis for monitoring and controlling work
7. To facilitate communications with stakeholders.

The project plan is expected to change over time as more information becomes known about the project and when changes in scope occur. Figure 3-25 is a sample annotated outline of the typical contents of each section.

There are many ways to organize the project plan, and not all sections are needed for every project. The format and approvals will usually differ from project to project unless the organization has developed common standards. The project plan does not have to be a large complex document, and for many projects it can be relatively short.

The project plan is another project management tool that is essential for effective project management. There is no "buy-in" issue. The concept and use of the project plan are fully accepted in mature PM organizations. The title page or inside front cover should include the signatures of the major stakeholders. The project manager signs the document representing the project team, who should have participated in the development of the document. The other important signatories are the heads of the functional organizations committed to support the project with resources and the sponsor/customer.

In establishing the project plan, the project manager cannot work alone. Participation is required from affected organizations and individuals. Often during the process of coordination and approval, negotiations may be needed to resolve schedule and budget issues and resource conflicts. The project manager, through negotiations, must resolve these conflicts in the best interests of the project.

NOTES

1. MIL-HDBK-881, *Work Breakdown Structures* (U.S. Department of Defense, 2 January 1998), paragraph 2.6.
2. Gregory T. Haugan, *Effective Work Breakdown Structures* (Vienna, VA: Management Concepts, Inc., 2002).
3. Quentin W. Fleming, *Put Earned Value (C/SCSC) Into Your Management Control System* (Worthington, OH: Publishing Horizons, Inc., 1983), p. 52.

FIGURE 3-25   Sample Project Plan Outline

PROJECT PLAN	
SECTION	CONTENTS
Title Page	Signatures of major stakeholders, especially functional managers and the sponsor/customer.
Project Charter	Update the project charter or the project manager's charter. Depending on contents of the charter, certain of the following sections may not be required.
Project Goals and Objectives	Describe the goals and objectives if they are not already defined in the project charter section. Include project justification and critical success factors.
Project Management Approach	Describe how the project will be managed, including meeting schedules, project reviews, reporting requirements and plans, tracking methodology, customer/sponsor interface. Include communication plans with stakeholders.
WBS*	Provide a detailed WBS and, if applicable, a WBS dictionary in an appendix.
Scope Statement or Statement of Work	Describe what work is planned. Organize the work by the WBS. Include a detailed work plan if relevant. Include a section on the project assumptions and planning and scheduling assumptions.
OBS with Assignments or Assignment Matrix*	Develop an organizational breakdown structure to identify responsibility for work. Alternatively, prepare a resource assignment matrix cross-referenced to the WBS. Alternatively, identify the responsibility for each activity or work package in the project management software.
Resource Plan*	Provide the project requirements for resources and document the commitments. This may include facilities, space, and equipment as well as key staff resources.
Master Schedule, Major Milestones, and Deliverables*	Include the master schedule baseline, including major milestones and deliverables. It should be in Gantt format but based on network planning.
Cost and Performance Baselines*	Include budgets by organization. If an earned value management system is used, include budgeted cost of work scheduled by WBS element and by organizational unit.
Risk Management Plan	Include an identification of risk elements and the risk response plan or a plan of how risk management will be accomplished.
Quality Management Plan	Describe how quality assurance and quality control will be accomplished.
Subsidiary Plans	Include other plans or summaries of plans as required by the project environment or customer (e.g., test plans, communication plans, public relation plans, staffing management plans).
Change Management	Discuss the procedures for making changes to the performance and cost and schedule baselines, including project scope and the approvals process.
Deliveries and Acceptance	Describe what needs to be done to deliver the product(s) to the customer and describe the acceptance or test procedures.
Close-out	Describe the close-out process, requirements, and responsibilities.
* These items may all be included in the project management software.	

CHAPTER 4

Advanced Planning and Scheduling Considerations

M uch effort has been put into scheduling methods and resource assignments as ways to improve schedule and resource allocation efficiency. These methods are also aimed at increasing the probability of projects being completed on time and within budget and performance constraints.

HEURISTICS AND OPTIMIZATION

Heuristics and optimization are two approaches to performing analyses and tradeoffs between time and resources:

- Heuristics involve the use of rules of thumb or approximations that have been shown to be reasonably effective. These are widely used.
- Optimization approaches seek a mathematical optimal solution and thus far have been limited to very small networks.

Resource-leveling Heuristics

Mathematical analysis (such as the network calculations described in Chapter 3) often produces a preliminary schedule that requires more resources during certain time periods than are available or requires changes in resource levels that are not manageable. Heuristics, such as those that allocate resources to activities on the critical path, can be applied to develop a schedule that reflects these constraints. Resource leveling using project management software often results in a project duration that is considerably longer than the preliminary schedule, although it does provide a solution to resource conflicts or overloading.

The most common decision rule in resource-leveling heuristics is to allocate resources to critical path activities first, then to the other paths depending on the heuristic chosen. In some project management software, there may be no choice in the matter. Some, for example, give priority to activities based on early start dates, and others give priority to the criticality or amount of slack. The more upscale project management software gives the user several options in choices of decision rules.

Resource leveling provides valuable information to the planner to assist in developing a workable schedule considering the availability of labor resources. A key aspect of critical chain project management is the heuristics used to allocate resources.

Crashing

Crashing is a mathematical technique used to compress the duration of projects while maintaining the planned scope. It is dependent upon data being available. Crashing was originally used only in construction projects because of the availability of data and the ability to perform the analyses necessary to develop the data. However, the concept has spread to other types of organizations.

Figure 4-1 presents the set of time and cost parameters for a single activity in a network. The "normal" data point represents the baseline plan data, and the "crash" data point represents the shorter time in which the activity could be performed if additional resources were added. These may be additional people, more work hours per day or per week, more productive people, etc. This analysis would be performed for activities that have not yet been started, and the project manager would select a combination of activities to crash that would result in the satisfactory compression of the schedule. Project costs are likely to increase.

PERT PROBABILITY AND MONTE CARLO

Chapter 3 discussed the determination of activity durations in PERT and presented definitions of the three time estimates, a, m, b—the optimistic, most likely, and pessimistic values. These data elements are used to determine the activity duration by using the formula: $t_e = (a + 4m + b)/6$. The network calculations using these activity durations show that the project duration is equal to the sum of the durations of the activities on the critical path.

There is another important aspect to using the three time estimates: They enable probability statements about the chances of meeting a specific schedule date. From the three time estimates, it is possible to establish probability estimates for each activity and for the project as a whole.

In developing the time estimates, the optimistic time is defined as that which could be met only about once in a hundred tries, and the pessimistic time as that which would be also required only about once in a hundred times. These correspond to probabilities of events occurring at the $\pm 3\sigma$ points, or three standard deviations in a frequency distribution.

FIGURE 4-1   Activity Normal and Crash Parameters

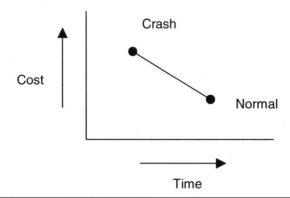

Because there are six standard deviations between these two points, PERT approximates the value of the standard deviation as one-sixth of the difference between the optimistic and the pessimistic estimates. In equation form, this is:

$$\sigma_{te} = (b - a)/6$$

This provides an indication of the spread of the distribution or an assessment of the risk in the estimate. The more confidence in the duration, the smaller the spread between a and b, and the smaller the standard deviation.

While activity durations along the critical path can be added to get the total duration of the project, it is not correct to add standard deviations. Variances, which are the squares of the standard deviations, are the terms that are added.

Figure 3-13 presented a classic PERT network of the sample project showing the three time estimates on the activities. Figure 4-2 is used to perform the PERT calculations. Only the critical path items from Figure 3-13 (and Figure 3-22) are shown.

Project Standard Deviation = (Square Root of the Sum of the Variances) = 1.79
95% Confidence Limit = 1.96 x (Project Standard Deviation) = 3.51

Figure 4-3 presents the data in graphic form on a timeline. Using the PERT activity data from the network diagram, the expected duration is 12.4 days. Also, there is a 95 percent probability that the project will be completed between approximately 9 days and 16 days from its start; there

FIGURE 4-2 PERT Calculations

PERT CALCULATION TABLE					
ACTIVITY	**TIME ESTIMATES**			**EXPECTED DURATION**	**VARIANCE**
	a	**m**	**b**	$\dfrac{a+4m+b}{6}$	$\dfrac{(b - a)^2}{36}$
Select New Appliances	1	2	4	2.17	0.25
Deliver New Appliances	6	8	16	9	2.78
Install Appliances	0.5	1	3	1.25	0.17
Column Totals:				12.42	3.2
				Project Expected Duration	**Project Total Variance**

is a 68 percent probability the project will be completed between 10.6 days and 14.3 days.

There are many criticisms of the PERT methodology (as compared to PDM). One of these is that on more complex projects, a path may become critical that has a much larger variance than the original critical path, and this schedule risk situation is not taken into account.

Monte Carlo methods are available that will have the computer run thousands of simulations taking into account all the variances in the various

FIGURE 4-3 PERT Calculation Probabilities

Kitchen Remodeling Project

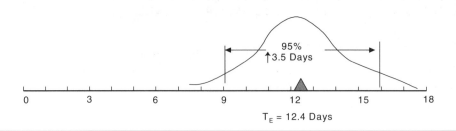

$T_E = 12.4$ Days

paths. These methods provide similar output to that in Figure 4-3 but are more mathematically correct. These programs are used for risk analyses on large projects where it is economic to get three relatively accurate time estimates for the activities.

CRITICAL CHAIN PROJECT MANAGEMENT

Thus, in certain aspects of CCPM, the methodology differs from the *PMBOK® Guide* standards. This section provides an overview of the planning process using CCPM.

CCPM has its own terminology. The planning process for developing a plan and schedule based on CCPM is similar to the seven-step procedure described in Chapter 3, which is repeated in Figure 4-4 for convenience. In the flow chart in Figure 4-5, the three major steps of CCPM replace Steps 4, 5, and 6 of the flow chart in Figure 4-4.

Step 4CC: Identify the Constraint—Critical Chain

In his book *Critical Chain*, as well as in his earlier book, *The Goal* (which focuses on production problems), Goldratt proposes a "Theory of Constraints" (TOC), which encourages managers to focus on the factors that prevent goals from being attained.[1] Using the TOC, Goldratt identifies the project constraint as: "the sequence of dependent events that prevents the project from completing in a shorter interval. Resource dependencies determine the critical chain as much as do activity dependencies."

Defining the principal constraint of a project in terms of the schedule derives from the impact the schedule has on project cost and project scope—the triple constraint. The importance of the schedule is discussed in Chapter 1.

As shown in the flow chart in Figure 4-5, the next step after the development of the network diagram is identifying the "critical chain." Because the resource constraint is often a significant project constraint, the TOC

FIGURE 4-4   Project Planning and Scheduling Process

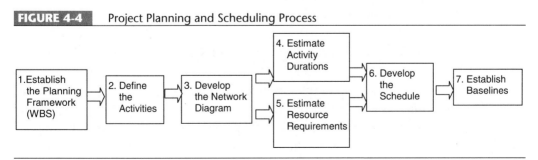

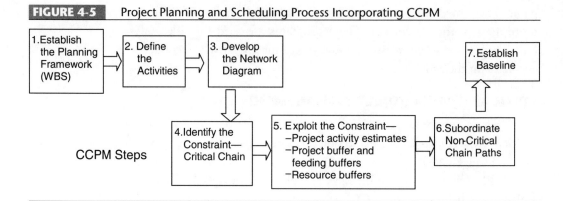

FIGURE 4-5 Project Planning and Scheduling Process Incorporating CCPM

method of project planning always considers it explicitly. Thus, the critical chain includes the resource dependencies that define the overall longest path (constraint) of the project. The methodology resolves all resource constraints in the process of determining the project critical chain.

The project may have gaps between activities on the critical path (chain) if a key resource is not available. If there are no resource constraints, the critical chain is the same initial activity path as the critical path. In either case, the CC project plan will differ from the "normal" deterministic critical path plan in philosophy, if not in fact.

Step 5CC: Exploit the Constraint

CCPM uses buffers in the establishment of the critical chain.

Project Activity Estimates

Activity estimating in CCPM was discussed in Chapter 3. There are three steps in the development of project activity estimates:

1. Preparing the plan with "low risk" estimates
2. Re-estimating using "average" or 50/50 estimates and reduced estimates
3. Collecting differences to develop buffers..

CCPM seeks to use the best estimate or 50 percent probable individual activity time estimates. (See Figure 3-14, Common Cause Variation Activity Duration, in Chapter 3.)

First, develop the plan using the normal low-risk (80–90 percent) activity estimates as provided by project personnel. Next (the order is important), solicit the estimated average or 50 percent probable estimates, assuming: (1) everything went as you hoped it would; (2) you have all necessary inputs at the start of each activity; and (3) you are able to devote 100 percent effort to the activity until it is finished.

Build the critical chain plan using these reduced duration time estimates.

Teach the estimators/workers to understand variation and the critical chain method, including assurance that they will not be criticized or otherwise affected either by over-running or under-running the estimated duration.

The third step is to collect the differences "Δt" between the low risk and the average estimates to develop buffers on each path (see Figure 3-14 in Chapter 3).

Buffers

The three types of buffers are:
- Project buffers
- Feeding buffers
- Resource buffers.

Project Buffers and Feeding Buffers—CCPM protects the overall project delivery time with a project buffer at the end of the critical chain. This protects the project from uncertainty regarding the individual activities on the critical activity path. Buffers appear as activities in the project schedule but have no work assigned to them.

The second type of buffer is called the "feeding buffer." Its purpose is to protect the critical chain with buffers at the end of feeding paths or paths that merge with the critical path (chain). This occurs wherever a non-critical chain activity joins the critical chain. This both protects the critical chain from disruptions on the activities feeding it and also allows critical chain activities to start early in case things go well. It also provides a means to measure the status of the feeding paths (by monitoring the size of the buffer) and keeps the primary focus on the activities in the critical chain.

When looking at activity durations and completion times from a probabilistic perspective, there are other considerations as well. Figure 4-6 illustrates a common relationship between activities in a PDM network.

Most projects have multiple activity paths, which merge into other paths and into the critical path by the end of the project. Many of these mergers occur toward the end of the project as groups of activities are completed.

Activity path mergers eliminate positive fluctuations and pass on only the longest delays. This follows the rule that an activity cannot start until all predecessor activities are completed. (If this is not the case, then the PDM chart is wrong and must be revised.)

FIGURE 4-6 Activity Path Merging

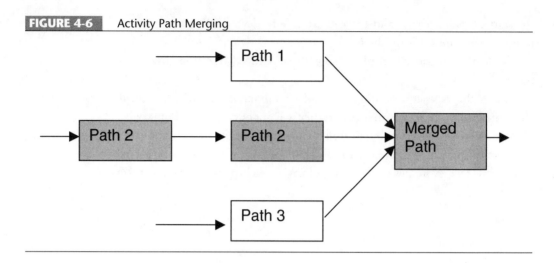

Look at the statistics of the situation depicted in Figure 4-6. If each of the last activities on paths 1, 2, and 3 has a 50 percent chance of completion within the estimated time, the probability that at least one will be late is more than 88 percent (1-.5*.5*.5). Or, if each individual probability of completion is as high as 90 percent, the probability of one being late is still 27 percent (1-.9*.9*.9). Experienced project managers are aware of this and closely monitor merging activity completions to increase the probability of overall on-time completion.

The advocates of CCPM have solutions for these problems:

1. Use the 50 percent time estimate for durations instead of the common 90 percent, but first get the 90 percent estimates.
2. Use the time saved to add buffers where paths merge and at the end of the project on the critical path (chain).
3. Modify the culture to encourage completing activities as rapidly as possible so that the successor activity can start as soon as possible.
4. Eliminate artificial intermediate schedule targets but focus on the end date and completing activities early.

Figure 4-7 illustrates the use of project and feeding buffers. The activities along Path 2 are the critical path or critical chain. Buffers are added to the merging paths and to the total project to protect from schedule slippage.

Several different approaches can be used to determine the size of the buffers:

1. They may be half of the sum of the differences between the 90 percent estimate and the 50 percent estimates, as shown on Figure 3-14 for the activities on the path.

FIGURE 4-7   CCPM Project and Feeding Buffers

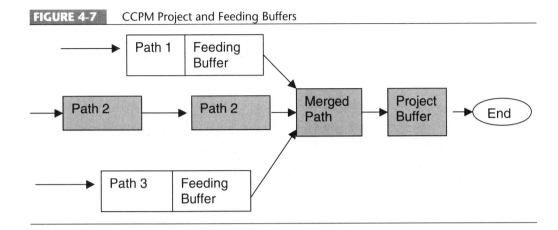

2. Goldratt suggests that the size of the feeding or project buffers be simply half of the sum of the unpadded or 50/50 activity durations on the chain of activities that precedes the buffer.

3. Others use a method developed by Lucent Technologies (per Leach) that sums the squares of the Δts and uses the square root of the sum to determine the buffer size.

4. Alternatively, some organizations use a factor based on experience that is applied to the duration of the path.

5. Another variation is to use two factors—one to account for the labor contingency and another to account for the "non-project loss time." The latter represents those items outside the project that can affect the schedule.

Resource Buffers—The third type of buffer, the resource buffer, does not take time in the critical chain. Resource buffers are intended to protect the critical chain from the unavailability of resources. They are placed wherever a resource has an assignment on the critical chain and the previous critical chain activity is performed by a different resource. Resource buffers are frequently flags to alert the project manager or the resource person or manager to make sure the resource is ready to work on the critical chain activities as soon as the activity input is ready. These may be in the form of "wake-up" calls 10, 5, and 2 days in advance.

Sometimes in high-risk situations and in subcontracts, it may be appropriate to include financial incentives in the resource buffers, such as paying for early delivery, penalizing for late delivery, or paying for standby time. This concept is based on the principle that the costs of a project delay due to unavailability of resources or subcontract delivery delay are much larger than the cost of ensuring that a key resource is available when needed on critical chain activities.

Resource buffers are used only on the critical chain activities; feeding buffers provide protection to non-critical activity chains.

Step 6CC: Subordinate Non-critical Chain Paths

Step 6 addresses the role of scheduling non-critical paths. The approach is to:

- Avoid early start schedules
- Use a late finish plan to:
  —reduce the impact of changes
  —delay project cash outlay
  —focus on the critical chain.

Early start schedules can reduce project risk by getting things done early, and most project management software programs have the early start as the default. Early start means that all of the non-critical path activities are scheduled to start as soon as possible, which is earlier than is necessary to meet the total project schedule date. People working on these activities are aware that there is slack in these activities and tend to take advantage of this situation.

CCPM uses a late start-late finish philosophy and an explicitly sized feeding buffer to protect the overall project from late completion of the feeding paths. Activities are scheduled to start as late as possible, considering the feeding buffer. The significant advantage of this approach lies in the ability of the project manager to focus on the critical chain activities and not be distracted by incidents in other, non-critical activities.

PROJECT MANAGEMENT MATURITY MODELS

Maturity models are used to identify where an organization's processes fall within industry-wide best practices. A project management maturity assessment provides the framework for a project management improvement program in the organization.

These models extend Deming's basic process control concepts: Organizations that control their processes can predict the characteristics of their products and services, predict their cost and schedules, and improve the effectiveness of operations.[2]

To improve project management processes and move up on the maturity scale, organizations typically must have defined business goals, be willing to establish a standard project management process, and have a commitment to project management. Goals must be specific, measurable, and attainable so that projects can be completed successfully following defined processes.

Figure 4-8 presents a generic model of a five-level system of project management maturity.

An assessment is performed to establish a baseline of where an organization fits in a scale of project management maturity. A typical assessment is based on a set of predetermined criteria prepared in the form of a checklist. To determine the maturity level of an organization, a thorough assessment covering each of the nine areas of the *PMBOK® Guide* is performed using a proprietary process. The results are evaluated and the ratings and recommendations tailored to the specific organization's culture, method of operation, and business environment.

Following is a generic set of definitions for a five-level scale of maturity describing the characteristics that might be found at each level, focusing only on planning and scheduling capability. These are an adaptation of the set used by LSM International in its PM staged maturity model.[3]

At Level I, the baseline level, project management, if practiced at all, is done in an ad-hoc manner throughout the organization. No standard processes and procedures are performed; standard tools and techniques are not used. Planning consists of only a Gantt chart schedule, although some managers may be using MS Project or some other software on their own.

At Level II, adapted level, project management practices are being introduced to the organization, and a project management methodology is

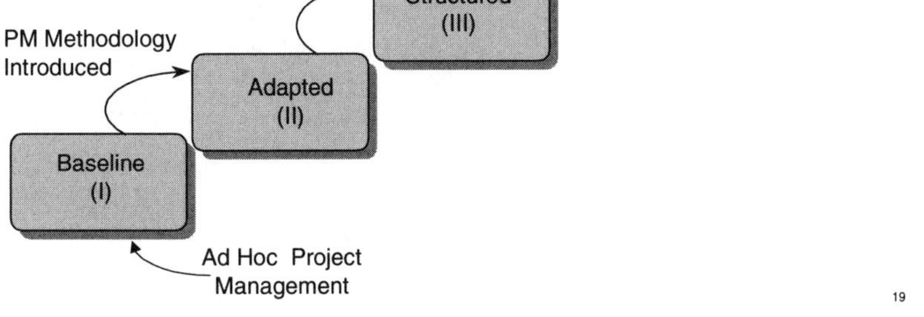

FIGURE 4-8   Generic Model—Levels of Project Management Maturity

being prepared. Project charters are prepared, as are WBSs. Project plans are prepared, approved, and issued, and a schedule baseline is established for projects using network planning techniques.

At Level III, structured level, project management principles and practices are accepted and used throughout the organization and documented in a company-wide methodology. A group is established as the focal point for project management methodology development and deployment. Documented procedures for time management are part of the organization's standard project management methodology. Resource planning and resource leveling are performed in conjunction with activity network planning. Earned value or critical chain methods and techniques are used on selected projects. Schedule performance is monitored as part of a schedule control system, and changes are formally administered.

At Level IV, integrated level, project management principles and practices are viewed in the organization as supportive and necessary to achieve business goals. The organization follows a "management by projects" philosophy. Portfolio management is performed to analyze and set priorities for projects. Earned value and other advanced techniques, including critical chain project management techniques, are used for time management. Planning and scheduling computer software is standardized. Schedule development and status reporting are performed across the company using a LAN or WAN or the Internet.

At Level V, synthesized level, project management practices are being continuously improved through a formal process, and project management activities are integrated into an Enterprise Project Management or Enterprise Resource Management system. The emphasis is on organizational and individual learning to increase project management effectiveness.

NOTES

1. Eliyahu M. Goldratt, *The Goal*, 2nd edition (Great Barrington, MA: The North River Press, 1992), p. 301.
2. W. Edwards Deming, *Out of the Crisis* (Cambridge, MA: Massachusetts Institute of Technology Center for Advanced Engineering Study, 1985).
3. Their model is described at: http://www.lsmzone.com.

CHAPTER 5

Summary and Checklist

Thchapter provides a review of the planning and scheduling process and includes a checklist to assist in developing effective work plans, resource plans, and schedules.

PLANNING AND SCHEDULING PROCESS REVIEW

Figure 5-1 repeats the seven steps necessary to develop an effective schedule for a project. The process is very logical. The activities to be performed are defined in Steps 1 and 2. Step 3 is the preparation of the network diagram using these activities. Steps 4 and 5 include the estimation of the duration of each activity and the resource requirements. From these data the schedule can be developed, with specific dates for each activity start and finish. Finally, after coordination with stakeholders, the baseline for implementing and controlling the project is established.

It doesn't matter whether the project is a multi-million dollar activity involving thousands of people or very small, involving a few people in an office—the steps are the same.

PLANNING AND SCHEDULING CHECKLIST

The checklist in Figure 5-2 is provided as a summary of the work to be performed in each of the seven steps. Assuming that you are going to

FIGURE 5-1   Project Planning and Scheduling Process

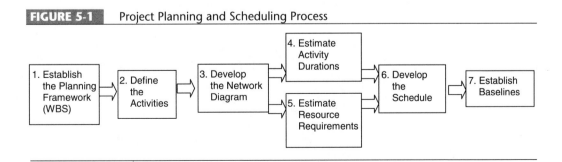

use project management software, experience has shown it is easier if you perform Steps 4 and 5 *before* Step 3 if you are using the Gantt display to enter data; the network elements are related to duration and show up as bars on the screen. The linkages identified in Step 3 are much easier to visualize when seen on the computer screen in Gantt format. Also, it often is easier to perform Steps 4 and 5 simultaneously because activity duration and resource assignment are closely related.

FIGURE 5-2   Checklist—Project Planning and Scheduling

YES	NO	QUESTIONS
		1. Establish the Planning Framework (WBS)
		Is there a list of project objectives?
		Is there a project charter?
		Is there a list of project deliverables?
		Is there a statement of work?
		Have you developed a WBS?
		Have you reviewed the WBS with your team?
		2. Define the Activities
		Have you entered the WBS into the project management software?
		Have you entered Project Management as the first WBS element at the top?
		If the Level 2 WBS elements have any logical flow (like phases), have you entered the WBS to match that flow?
		Have you indented the various levels to match the WBS levels?
		Have you entered the deliverables as milestones under the appropriate WBS element?
		Have you identified deliverable milestones by making them zero duration?
		Have you established a "start" milestone? (Or "contract award" under Project Management?)
		Have you identified meetings and reports under Project Management?
		Have you added notes to yourself of things to remember or contractual dates or commitments in the activity note field?
		Have you listed the activities as verb-noun combinations or verb-adjective-noun combinations under each lowest level WBS element?
		Have you identified critical control points and metrics to use for performance measurement?
		Does each of the activities meet the applicable criteria?
		3. Develop the Network Diagram
		Does every activity (except the start milestone) have one or more predecessors identified?
		Does every activity (except the finish milestone or independent deliverables) have one or more successors identified?
		4. Estimate Activity Durations (often performed simultaneously with Step 5 of the process flow chart)
		Are all the activity durations to be estimated in this step of fixed duration? (Effort driven activity durations are often more easily estimated in Step 5.)
		Have you estimated the duration of all the fixed-duration activities?
		5. Estimate Resource Requirements
		Have you set up the beginnings of a resource table with codes and labor rates and cost elements?
		Have the resources on fixed-duration activities been assigned using percentages or work hours?
		Have you identified the number of person-hours or person-days for each effort-driven activity?
		Have you identified the number and code of persons assigned to each effort-driven activity?
		Are all milestones shown as zero-duration activities?
		Have you assigned resources to all the activities?
		6. Develop the Schedule
		Does the overall schedule fit within the required or desired duration?
		Do you know which are the critical path activities?
		Have you reviewed the individual activities on the critical path to eliminate cushion and reduce the overall project duration to meet schedule requirements?
		Have you reworked the network logic to reduce overall duration (e.g., planned certain activities to be performed in parallel rather than in series)?
		Have you reduced scope to meet project schedule demands?
		Have you checked for resource conflicts?
		Have you used resource leveling to eliminate conflicts?

continues

FIGURE 5-2   continued

YES	NO	QUESTIONS
		Have you made resource changes and/or plan changes to eliminate conflicts and to meet overall project schedule requirements?
		Have you checked to see if the total cost is within the budget?
		Have you performed schedule-resource-scope tradeoffs to meet schedule-cost-resource-performance requirements?
		Has your team been assisting you in these rework activities?
		Have you reviewed the resulting schedule, budget, and resource requirements with your project team?
		Have you reviewed the resulting schedule, budget, and resource requirements with the project sponsor or customer?
7. Establish Baselines		
		Have you reviewed the schedule, budget, and resource requirements with the functional managers you are looking to for support?
		Have the functional managers "signed off" on your plan?
		Have you formally established the schedule baseline?
		Are you ready to issue work authorizations?
		Have you distributed the project plan or schedules and budgets?
		Have you issued work authorizations and budgets?
		Have you started work on implementing the plans?

Bibliography

Anthony, Robert N. *Planning and Control Systems: A Framework for Analysis* (Boston: Harvard University Graduate School of Business Administration, 1965).

Associated General Contractors. *CPM in Construction: A Manual for General Contractors* (Washington, D.C.: Associated General Contractors, 1965).

Carroll, Lewis. *The Complete Works of Lewis Carroll* (New York: The Modern Library, Random House, 1922).

Clark, C. The Optimum Allocation of Resources among Activities of a Network, *Journal of Industrial Engineering* 1961; 12 (January-February): 11–17.

Deming, W. Edward. *Out of the Crisis* (Cambridge, MA: Massachusetts Institute of Technology Center for Advanced Engineering Study, 1985).

Fleming, Quentin W. *Put Earned Value (C/SCSC) Into Your Management Control System* (Worthington, OH: Publishing Horizons, Inc., 1983).

Fulkerson, D. A Network Flow Computation for Project Cost Curves, *Management Sciences* 1961; 7.

Goldratt, Eliyahu M. *Critical Chain* (Great Barrington, MA: The North River Press Publishing Corporation, 1997).

Goldratt, Eliyahu M. *The Goal*, 2nd edition. (Great Barrington, MA: The North River Press, 1992).

Goodstein, Leonard, Timothy Nolan, and J. William Pfeiffer. *Applied Strategic Planning: A Comprehensive Guide* (San Diego: Pfeiffer & Co., 1992).

Haugan, Gregory T. *Effective Work Breakdown Structures* (Vienna, VA: Management Concepts, Inc., 2002).

Haugan, Gregory T. *PERT* (Baltimore, MD: Martin Marietta Aerospace Division, 1962).

Haugan, Gregory T. *Primer—Project Management Methodology* (Heathsville, VA: GLH, Inc., 1998).

Iannone, Anthony L. *Management Program Planning and Control with PERT, MOST and LOB* (Englewood Cliffs, N.J.: Prentice-Hall, Inc., 1967).

Kelley, J. Critical Path Planning and Scheduling: Mathematical Basis, *Operations Research* 1961; vol. 9(3): 296–321.

Kerzner, Harold. *Project Management: A Systems Approach to Planning, Scheduling, and Controlling*, 7th edition (New York: John Wiley & Sons, 2001).

Koontz, Harold and Cyril O'Donnell. *Principles of Management*, 2nd edition (New York: McGraw-Hill Book Company, Inc., 1959).

Leach, Lawrence P. *Critical Chain Project Management* (Boston: Artech House, Inc., 2000).

Lock, Dennis, ed. *Project Management Handbook* (Aldershot, England: Gower Technical Press, Ltd., 1987).

Malcolm, D.G., J.H. Roseboom, C.E. Clark, and W. Fazar. Application of a Technique for Research and Development Program Evaluation, *Operations Research* 1959; 7(5).

Martino, R.L. *Finding the Critical Path* (New York, American Management Association, 1964).

Meredith, Jack R., and Samuel J. Mantel, Jr. *Project Management, A Managerial Approach*, 3rd edition (New York: John Wiley & Sons, 1995).

MIL-HDBK-881, *Work Breakdown Structures* (U.S. Department of Defense, 2 January 1998).

Miller, Robert W. *Schedule, Cost and Profit Control with PERT* (New York: McGraw-Hill Book Company, Inc., 1963).

Office of Naval Material. Line of Balance Technology (Department of the Navy: NAVEXOS P 1851, 24 February 1958).

Project Management Institute. *A Guide to the Project Management Body of Knowledge (PMBOK® Guide)* (Newton Square, PA: Project Management Institute, 2000).

Rosenau, Milton D., Jr. *Project Management for Engineers* (Belmont, CA: Lifetime Learning Publications, 1984).

Rosenau, Milton D., Jr. *Successful Project Management*, 3rd edition (New York: John Wiley & Sons, Inc., 1998).

Webster's New World Dictionary of the American Language, College Edition (New York: The World Publishing Company, 1966).

Index